Some Contemporary
Americans

THE UNIVERSITY OF CHICAGO PRESS
CHICAGO, ILLINOIS

—

THE BAKER & TAYLOR COMPANY
NEW YORK

THE CAMBRIDGE UNIVERSITY PRESS
LONDON

THE MARUZEN-KABUSHIKI-KAISHA
TOKYO, OSAKA, KYOTO, FUKUOKA, SENDAI

THE MISSION BOOK COMPANY
SHANGHAI

Some Contemporary Americans

THE PERSONAL EQUATION IN LITERATURE

By Percy H. Boynton

The University of Chicago Press
Chicago · Illinois

4431
810.4

Composed and Printed By
The University of Chicago Press
Chicago, Illinois, U.S.A.

419973

TO
L. D. B.

Acknowledgment

ELEVEN of these essays, the second to the twelfth, were printed in the *English Journal* from September, 1922, to June, 1924. The first originally appeared in the *Nation*, and the last in the *Literary Review*. The remaining three contain in part material drawn from contributions to the *Dial*, the *Freeman*, the *Independent*, and the *New Republic*, to all which periodicals acknowledgment is hereby gratefully made.

PERCY H. BOYNTON

Contents

I

American Neglect of American Literature

WHEN the wise Dr. Georg Brandes, visited the United States some years ago, he was quoted as saying soon after he landed that he did not propose to be interviewed any more about the works of Emerson, Whitman, and Poe, because nobody over here had read them. He was not quoted as expressing any wonder at this, but simply as stating what he had observed. If he did wonder—if perhaps he inquired how it was possible for the educated American to know so little about the best of American literature—his wonder doubtless grew when he found that an American could go through the forms of being educated without ever hearing of American literature after entrance into high school, and that, however much he might care to, it was rarely possible for him to indulge in any intensive study of his native literature under school, college, or even university auspices. If the alert guest was as wide awake as usual, and went on to ask why this surprising fact could be, it is doubtful if he received a good offhand explanation.

The reason is that to answer such a question, a good apologist would have needed to start, like Lowell's organist,

Beginning doubtfully and far away,

and when he had built the bridge from a far past would have needed, if he were candid, to admit that there was no valid defense for the present, and content himself with simply explaining. He would have had to consider two persistent and mutually provocative facts in American life: that American culture has always been timidly self-conscious, and that American literature has always been neglected in the American college; and to recognize that the college is the product of American intellectual tradition and also the chief determinant of America's intellectual bias in the year after next; and he must, therefore, have explained what the college has included in the course of study and what it has left out, by an account of college evolution and of community thinking.

I

Within the college the status of American literature, until day before yesterday, has quite evidently rested on a piece of natural, rather than directed, development. It can best be explained in its disjunction with the status of American history, for this subject receives quite all the attention it deserves. Somehow or other, we may indolently say— although the Bancroft-Parkman-Prescott tradition is at the basis of it—the leadership in the study of history on this side of the Atlantic is very largely in the hands of scholars in the American field. In consequence, the story of the United States is well and abundantly expounded, and college graduates in large numbers carry away that partial and partially useful knowledge which comes from

[3]

the exclusive study of political, economic, and military annals. Yet the leadership in the study of literature on this side of the Atlantic, because of the influence of German methods of scholarship, is rightfully enough in the hands of pre-Shakespearean scholars. As a consequence, again, English literature is variously presented, but—perhaps all unconsciously—the earlier periods have been stressed as most worthy of study, the best maturing scholarship has been diverted toward them, and American literature has in many quarters been either slighted or explicitly discredited.

Thus, in graduate instruction, the study of special American schools, special tendencies, and special genera has been attempted up to this time only in isolated cases. Nevertheless, the material is at hand. The older libraries, through mere automatic accumulation, have acquired great stores of unstudied material; and a certain few collections of the richest interest lie serenely undisturbed by the investigator. In writing the history of our country—even the ostensibly literary history

—the social satires, the secondary fiction, and the history of the stage have been almost as completely forgotten by the historians as by the general public. Still the colleges do not seize their opportunity. Not one eminent university man in this country today has devoted his whole career to studying or teaching the literary history of America.

The immediate consequences of this are the obvious ones on which Professor Brandes remarked. In the secondary schools, American authors are read more or less, though decreasingly when college-entrance examinations loom up as the determining influence. Yet the school children have to be taught American literature out of the fulness of the heart rather than out of the fulness of the mind, for the teachers have seldom enjoyed any special training. The average receptive college graduates who are going into business or into professions other than teaching —even the ones with so-called literary inclinations—very rarely discover for themselves the drift of national thought as it might have been presented in historical courses.

Every other literature but our own is so studied, but it has never been the fashion for educated Americans to take American literature seriously. It has not been done in the best academic circles.

II

Academic inertia, however, is not the only factor in the equation. A much more important one is the academic timidity which reflects the mind of the country. The American reading public has all along failed to appreciate that, even though we are fortunate in the enormous heritage which a sharing in English speech and English feeling has given us, we have also an immediate possession, not by heritage, but by the right of eminent domain; that the literature of our own land is ours to understand and build upon; that it expresses us as no literature from across the seas can do; that a knowledge of ourselves depends upon an intimate acquaintance with the American stock quite as much as on an analysis of the English soil from which it sprang.

The deference of the American intellect and the American college is well rooted in history. Cambridge University furnished the New England tradition for the colonial centuries. With the development of a national consciousness, commencement speakers began to orate loosely about the "rising glories of America." For a generous half-century after the Revolution, aspiring young America looked to itself for the new poets and prophets of the New World. This was a natural display of exaggerated provincialism; and a natural feature of it was that all the time aspirants were most anxiously listening for any applause that might come over from London. No wonder that in those early stages young America was superficially imitative of the popular English models; no wonder Dennett said of Fitz-Greene Halleck what he might have said of any other Knickerbocker—that it was hard for him to forget himself, for "when he forgot himself he had to forget so many people." From 1820 on, Irving, Cooper, Bryant, and their followers protested more and more frequently against a certain condescension in foreigners to which Lowell addressed himself in his essay of 1865. Yet all these men, and cultured America as a whole, played up to this condescension, and encouraged it by evidently expecting it; stimulated it by the peevish feebleness of their protests. Lowell himself was always apologetic, always hoping to gain confidence in his countrymen. Charles Eliot Norton was deferent toward all things British or European, and felt for the crudities of American life a distress which was only a refinement upon the snobbishness of the Effinghams in Cooper's *Homeward Bound* and *Home as Found*.

The fact is that the refined American of the mid-nineteenth century was afraid to contemplate the incarnation of America. He knew that Uncle Sam was too mature for it; he feared that it was like Tom Sawyer; he did what he could to mold it into the image of little Lord Fauntleroy. And he apologized for Whitman. When Mark Twain visited William Dean Howells in Cambridge in 1871, they were both young sojourners

from what was to Cambridge an undiscrimi-
nated West. Young Mr. Clemens did not care
at all so far as he himself was concerned, but
he cared a great deal in behalf of his friend,
who was so incorrigibly western. And in
recording his solicitude, he recorded a striking fact of that generation: that American
culture was afraid even of American phenomena which Europe approved. "I did not
care," said Mr. Howells of Mr. Clemens, "to
expose him to the critical edge of that Cambridge acquaintance which might not have
appreciated him at, say, his transatlantic
value."

III

Whatever could once have been said in
defense of such a situation has now lost its
virtue. For, in spite of the increasingly
urgent need that America should come to
some understanding of herself, the colleges
have done little more than before the war
with Spain to contribute to any literary
introspection. They have presented formal
American history very well; they may have
presented economics better; but they have

gained but little ground in their treatment of the literature. No one in this century has surpassed the work in the last of Tyler and Richardson in general history, or of the authors of the leading volumes in the "American Men of Letters" series.

All of which has become a matter of no small importance in American life. For we have reached the point where, as a community, we must at last be able to think clearly in terms of international relations, and where, as a first step toward any clarity of thought, we must have some clear and unified approximation, not merely as to our "manifest destiny," but as to what we are and what the American concept of the state should be. And these findings, if they are to amount to anything at all, must be based on a knowledge of the course of American thought as related to the thought of the world. The army and navy, the legislatures, and the market—these are, after all, only symptoms. The vital points are what the nation has been thinking and what it has been failing to think.

Considered in this light, American literature makes an imperative claim on the
national attention. Silas Pettijohn may very
properly feel his own shortcomings in the
presence of Shakespeare, but it is a duty as
well as a right of Silas Pettijohn to know his
own mind. This is something that America
has yet to learn. There need be no question
for the self-derogatory American as to the
comparative merits of Cooper and Scott,
Longfellow and Tennyson, Emerson and
Carlyle; but there should be much question
as to what Cooper and Irving meant three
generations ago, why Willis thrived and Poe
languished, what the Transcendentalists sig-
nified, how vital was the contribution of
Cambridge to the life of the nation, where
Whitman triumphed and how he failed, and
who took up the torch when the elders laid
it down.

Out of an educational policy which will
recognize this need, a policy extended to the
leading universities and colleges, and persisted in for years, there ought to come two
contrasting results. One is that through an

acquaintance with our native writers the educated American will both enrich and modify his feeling for American history. In the past he has condemned much of our literature because it was too imitative, and discredited the rest because it was not imitative enough, largely for the reason that he was not really familiar with either the exotic or the indigenous parts of it. Yet in them together are the secret and the riches of our national tradition and character. It cannot be too emphatically stated that the intrinsic value of American literature must to American students be a matter of secondary importance. What the public has wanted in any generation is vitally significant as a question of literary history. If our spokesmen have been great, well and good. If they have been little, it is ours to understand the littleness, for in them the national character has for the moment been expressed. What Professor Shorey wrote some years ago of American scholarship was directly—if not then explicitly—to this point:

The superior culture of Oxford or Paris . . . . is due to the background of the national tradition in language and literature, *and the controlling consciousness of the tradition* in the minds of teachers and taught.

Deliberately to train our most highly schooled group of thinkers in total disregard of the essentially national aspect of this tradition is to assume that the needs of the student in the United States are identical with those of the student in the British Isles or in Canada or in Australia.

Under "the controlling consciousness of this tradition" will come the further result that through the schools—already in this respect more enlightened than the colleges, because less self-conscious—the acquaintanceship of the children with the American classics will become more intelligent in recognition of their native quality. Not one in a hundred now could comment thus to any purpose on "Maud Muller," or "Snowbound," or "The Bridge," or even *The Last of the Mohicans*. To foster in a whole generation some clear recognition of other qualities in America than its bigness, and of other distinctions between the past and the present than that they are far apart, is to contribute toward the consciousness of a national individuality which is the first essential of national life. Such a task would be needful enough if America were peopled with native Americans. With the population as it is, such education is far more important than in any other land; and yet it can be attempted only when the teachers of English are trained to know the spirit and content of American letters.

I want not to damage the case by overstating it. There has already been a great deal of profitable study of American literature, the fruits of which have often been put into print. Several well-known college teachers offer occasional survey courses, and a growing number of younger men are doing a more serious kind of work. But in the colleges American literature has no real footing in comparison with the footing of either American history or English literature. Just now, however, the American periodicals addressed to thoughtful people are telling us in issue after issue that we must put our minds upon ourselves, that we must look to our past, and to our present, and then intelligently to our future. We who read these periodicals admit the charge gravely—and then read more such articles. If we are deeply affected, we remark that somebody ought to do something about it. We may go on in this course for years without getting anywhere, if this is all we do. The mind of the nation cannot be generally influenced by the articles in a few weeklies or monthlies of small circulation. Some other machinery must be set in motion—machinery which is continuously operative among the millions: of course, the educational system of the country. This system is already doing much, but one among many more things it can do is to present our national literature as an index of the national mind; and the further steps in any real progress must be taken by the colleges.

II

Edwin Arlington Robinson

I

IN THE year 1891, when Edward Arlington Robinson entered Harvard, readers of
poetry in English were all keenly aware
of the passing of the best-known Victorian
singers. They were recalling Emerson's
"Terminus" and Longfellow's "Ultima
Thule," Whitman's "November Boughs"
and Whittier's "A Lifetime," Tennyson's
"Crossing the Bar," and Browning's "Aso-
lando." No group were ready at once to succeed the popular oracles. Not a single poet
who was in his prime between 1890 and 1900
is being widely read today. And that decade
recognized its own poverty. People had more
reason than usual to sing the perennial refrain
of "the good old days," and to prophesy
that it would be long before the world saw
their equal.

[16]

The livelier spirit of the times was expressed by a number of young rebels against Victorianism who were noisily assertive on their favorite theme of "art for art's sake." They were occupied in composing intricate and ingenious verses. They were engrossed, like Masters' "Petit the Poet," in inditing

Triolets, villanelles, rondels, rondeaus,
Seeds in a dry pod, tick, tick, tick,
Tick, tick, tick, what little iambics,
While Homer and Whitman roared in the pines!

Some of them did "pastels in prose," and many edited ephemeral little periodicals following on the *Yellow Book* and the *Chap Book*, like the *Lark* and *Truth in Boston*, fourteen of which sprouted, bloomed, and withered in the United States during the first half of 1897. Probably the only lines in any of them recalled by the readers of today are Gelett Burgess' ironic jibe at new art in his quatrain on the purple cow.

From the vantage point of today one can see that four men of genuine power were growing steadily at the time in fulfilment of Longfellow's "Possibilities," each "an admiral sailing the high seas of thought," in contrast to the little canoeists who were having their regatta in the popular magazines. Of these, Richard Hovey (1865–1900) and William Vaughn Moody (1869–1910) died before reaching middle age; but Edgar Lee Masters and Edwin Arlington Robinson, both born in the same year with Moody, are even now in mid-career. Both published before 1900 and neither was recognized till long after. Just how fast has been the speed of the literary current in these latter years is indicated by three recent books on American poetry. Miss Rittenhouse's *The Younger American Poets* (1904) includes eighteen authors, all but five of whom were born before the conclusion of the Civil War. Miss Lowell's *Tendencies in Modern American Poetry* (1917) includes six poets, none of whom were mentioned in the earlier book, and the oldest of whom was Robinson. In Louis Untermeyer's *The New Era in American Poetry* (1919), of sixteen poets named in chapter headings only three were born before 1875, and Robinson again is the oldest.

Edwin Arlington Robinson

So rapid a change in the make-up of the modern choir has led to various cheap and easy generalizations by the kind of people who would rather talk about literature than read it. They refer loosely and mistakenly to contemporary poetry as if all the verse of today were of one kind, and all of it characterized by defiant revolt against old forms and old ideas. It is true enough that experiment and innovation are being tried in all fields of art at present. In music Debussy and Schoenberg, in painting Cezanne and Matisse, in staging and costuming Craig and Bakst, have shocked and surprised quite as many as they have edified, and have given rise to the same sort of querulous protest indulged in by those who speak as if all modern poetry belonged to the school of Alfred Kreymborg and "Anne Knish." Yet in poetry[1] most of the recent work has not been wantonly bizarre, most of the more distinguished verse

[1] For an approach to the whole question of modern poetry, the following books are useful: General discussions: Max Eastman, *Enjoyment of Poetry*, 1913; J. L. Lowes, *Convention and Revolt in Poetry*, 1919; W. A. Neilson, *The Essentials of Poetry*, 1912. Specific criticism: Conrad Aiken, *Scepticisms: Notes on Contemporary Poetry*, 1919;

has not been "free," and all but one of the men and women who have had anything genuine to say in free verse have also mastered and used the conventional verse forms.

II

Mr. Robinson is an emphatic illustration of the fact that modernity in art does not depend on strangeness or newness. His subject-matter has no word of modern movements in it. The residents of his Tilbury are apparently men and women of today, but the qualities that make them humanly alive are constants in human life. Change a few allusions and you may put them as far back in history as you choose. On the other hand, his use of Arthurian material is not in any limited sense "historical." He turned to the stories of Merlin and Launcelot because their stories were full of the elements that make up life today. He had no interest in "recon-

---

Amy Lowell, *Tendencies in Modern American Poetry*, 1917; Louis Untermeyer, *The New Era in American Poetry*, 1919. Collections: Monroe and Henderson, *The New Poetry, an Anthology*, 1917; Lloyd R. Morris, *The Young Idea (An Anthology of Opinion)*, 1917; Louis Untermeyer, *Modern American Poetry*, 1921; Marguerite Wilkinson, *New Voices*, 1919.

structing the past"; rather he turned to the past in order to get away from things to people and to avoid the distraction of modern realism. Pullman cars, up-to-date hotels, country clubs, and Fifth Avenue palaces were too likely to compete in interest with the human experiences on which he wanted to concentrate attention. Ben Jonson in his soliloquy on Shakespeare, as Robinson imagines it, is a friend and neighbor of the bard of Avon, but he talks of the qualities in the dramatist which might be found in any genius of today or of tomorrow. Only in his two prose plays, *The Porcupine* and *Van Zorn* —his least effective writings—does Mr. Robinson write of specific twentieth-century people living in a definitely twentieth-century world. On the whole he feels that we of today are fighting perhaps better than our fathers,

> Yet we shall have our darkness, even as they,
> And there shall be another tale to tell.

It is not only in time that his characters are detached. They are like the stars to the average man—in the control of some vast system, but little related each to each; and many are falling stars. Flammond, who is a sort of mendicant, even though a princely one, comes from God knows where, pours out the milk of human kindness in Tilbury town, and passes beyond the horizon. Captain Craig, "abhorred iconoclast," dying impoverished, bequeaths God's universe and a largess of philosophy to the friends he is leaving. Miniver Cheevy hates commonplace, despises the gold he does not own, and thinks, and drinks. It is Richard Cory and Avon, both endowed with possession and position, who die before their time, one by his own hand, and the other in a mania of fear.

If the characters are unlocated in time and space it follows of course that there is a little "local color" in Mr. Robinson's work, and almost nothing of background picture. If the reader can occasionally supply a kind of drop curtain against which to see one of Mr. Robinson's characters, the details are supplied as by a producer for a playwright.

But here any comparison with playwright should stop; for the poems have as little in the way of detailed incidents as they do of tableaus. Perhaps it is because of this subjective quality that his two prose plays achieved no stage success, that there was too little in them to meet the eye of the spectator, or at least too large an element of subjective subtlety. Mr. Robinson's literary matter is compounded of people who are four parts intellect to one part emotion. They are real characters because of the fire in their souls; but most of them have no physical embodiment, except as the reader supplies it, just as he supplies the backgrounds for them.

This, when one stops to think of it, is extraordinary material from which to make poetry, for it is the essence of most poetry that it is concretely picturesque, that it deals with "the stuff of life," and that the truth inherent in that stuff shall be brought home somehow and not too aggressively to the reader. If one inclines to challenge Mr. Robinson on this ground, or the admirer of

Mr. Robinson (since his own refusal to defend himself has been made once for all in "Dear Friends"), the only reply to offer is that poetry cannot be ruled out of court on technicalities. If there is a discrepancy between a genuine poem and a definition, it is the definition that suffers. What makes Mr. Robinson an unchallengeable poet is that he writes movingly of the spirit of man. It is only incidentally interesting that he puts this spirit not in conflict with social or economic forces but in conflict with its own hopes and fears and desires. As a British critic has recently written:

> Mr. Robinson is in the true Greek tradition in this, that, whereas most of his fellow-countrymen who are poets see man beset by society, which is circumstance, he sees man beset by his own character, which is fate.

Yet of course one can go farther in this case, and far enough to show, through the allusions already made to background and character, that if Mr. Robinson does not paint, he puts brush and palette in the hands of his readers, and inspires them to give local habitations to the spirits he creates.

III

Again there is nothing strange or ultra-modern in the manner of his writing. Throughout his work he has used conventional rhythms and stanza forms—in the longer poems mainly blank verse, in the shorter ones stanzas of from four to eight lines with three, four, or five stresses. Yet these measures become his own as he uses them. His work as a whole has a character, and many of his lines are unmistakably his own and none other's, with a certain almost extreme yet unlabored precision, coupled often with a gleam of humor or a touch of passion. His style is like the people of his creation, dominantly intellectual, but touched with emotion.

"I never touch a spigot nowadays,"
He said, and raised the glass up to his lips,
"But I thank God for orchards."

"Flammond" is full of these etched passages:

What he needed for his fee
To live, he borrowed graciously.

His mien distinguished any crowd.
His credit strengthened when he bowed.

What broken link
Withheld him from the destinies
That came so near to being his?

In a measure, though not to the point of
monotony, Mr. Robinson could say with his
own Captain Craig:

For I do nought,
Say nought, but with an ancient levity
That is the forbear of all earnestness.

IV

In view of this earnestness which is apparent through all his work, it is a little surprising that he has not been more actively
assailed by that group of the ultra-moderns
who have revived the cry of "art for art's
sake," and hold that if a poet have any moral
convictions he ought at least to keep quiet
about them—the group corresponding to
those who were making the welkin ring
with the same cry when Mr. Robinson was
first writing in the 1890's. Probably one
reason that the smart set have let him alone
is that they have seen so clearly that not to
begin the assault showed the discretion that

is the better part of valor. And at the same
time they may have been disarmed by something in him that they are in the habit of
calling "healthy pessimism," although by
that phrase they mean nothing more than a
willingness to admit that all is not well with
the world.

Beyond question all is not well with Mr.
Robinson's world. The people in it who
interest him most are adjudged failures by
the great majority who worship success.
The "Tilbury tune," which is the tune of the
Philistines, has a false note in it.

> A note that able-bodied men might sound
> Hosannas on while Captain Craig lay quiet.
> They might have made *him* sing by feeding him
> Till he should march again, but probably
> Such yielding would have jeopardized the rhythm.

Harder to bear in this world, however, than
a moral squint in the blundering crowd is
the fact that man is born to trouble as the
sparks fly upward.

> "Bedivere,"
> Began the solid host, "you may as well
> Say now as at another time hereafter

That all your certainties have bruises on 'em,
And all your pestilent asseverations
Will never make a man a salamander—
Who's born, we are told, so fire won't bite him."

Nevertheless, he does not despair in the face of evil.

Because one half of humankind
Lives here in hell, shall not the other half
Do any more than just for conscience' sake
Be miserable? Is this the way for us
To lead these creatures up to find the light,
Or the way to be drawn down to find the dark
Again?

Captain Craig is the key poem to Mr. Robinson's philosophy. It is a poem of childhood, sunlight, laughter, and hope declaimed by an indomitable old vagabond of eternity who is invincible in death, and is fittingly borne to the grave while the trombones of the Tilbury band blare the "Dead March" in *Saul*. The Captain is in a way Mr. Robinson let loose, stripped of all verbal restraint. His type is never restrained (as the poet Robinson is reported to be in ordinary intercourse). Men of his kind are extrava-

gant of time, of gesture, of vocal and rhetor-
ical emphasis, of words themselves. Out of
the abundance of their hearts their mouths
speak all sorts of irresponsible, whimsical,
exalted, splendid speculation. Captain Craig
is in a word self-expression in very being, and
condemns in joyous scorn the man who
believes that life is best fulfilled through
discipline and renunciation. Instead he offers
something positive:

> It is the flesh
> That ails us, for the spirit knows no qualm,
> No failure, no down-falling; so climb high
> And having set your steps regard not much
> The downward laughter clinging at your feet,
> Nor overmuch the warning; only know
> As well as you know dawn from lantern-light
> That far above you, for you, and within you,
> There burns and shines unwavering
> And always yours, the truth. Take on yourself
> But your sincerity, and you take on
> Good promise for all climbing; fly for truth,
> And hell shall have no storm to crush your flight,
> No laughter to vex down your loyalty.

This is the note through all Mr. Robinson's poems and plays. His disbelief in

negativism leads him often to be impatient and caustic, and leads the cloudy-minded to timid deprecation of what they think is his cynicism, not knowing the difference between this and irony. Mr. Robinson is never cynical toward the things that are more excellent. He is only convinced that people's mistaken convictions as to what is more excellent result in a perverted estimate; he is only attempting to substitute light for shadow, laughter for gloom; he is only saying with Larry Scammon in *The Porcupine:*

> Stop me if I am too cheerful; but at the same time, if I can instil the fertile essence of Hope into this happy household, for God's sake let me do it. . . . . You had better—all of you—begin to get yourselves out of your own light, and cease to torment your long-bedevilled heads with the dark doings of bogies that have no real existence.

What such bogies can accomplish if they are not banished is told in the terrible story of *Avon's Harvest.*

Mr. Santayana's comment on William James may very properly be applied to the creator of Captain Craig:

Edwin Arlington Robinson

He would let fall golden words, picturesque, fresh
from the heart, full of the knowledge of good and evil.
Incidentally there would crop up some humorous
characterization, some candid expression of doubt or
of instinctive preference, some pungent scrap of learning; radicalism plunging sometimes into the subsoil of
all human philosophies; and, on occasion, thoughts of
simple wisdom and wistful piety, the most unfeigned
and manly that anybody ever had.

BIOGRAPHICAL NOTE

Edwin Arlington Robinson was born in 1869 at
Head Tide, Maine, and lived during boyhood in
Gardiner, Maine, to which his poems often allude as
"Tilbury." He entered Harvard in 1891, withdrew
early in his course, and later went to New York, where
he prospered no better than one would conventionally
expect of a poet. From 1905 to 1910 he held a position
in the New York Custom House on the appointment of
President Roosevelt. Although he had published three
volumes of poetry by the end of the latter year, it was
not until 1915 and the second publishing of *Captain
Craig*, which had first appeared in 1902, that he gained
general recognition. Since that year he has held un-
questioned place in the first rank of living poets. He
has left his native state and now lives in Brooklyn,
New York. Here he is on the edge of the great stream
of events, but has never been submerged by them. His
work has not taken on the tone of the metropolis in

Some Contemporary Americans

any particular. He was awarded the Pulitzer Prize for the best volume of American poetry in 1921, his *Collected Poems*.

Mr. Robinson's publications in verse are as follows: *The Children of the Night*, 1897; *Captain Craig*, 1902; *The Town down the River*, 1910; *The Man against the Sky*, 1916; *Merlin*, 1917; *Launcelot*, 1920; *The Three Taverns*, 1920; *Avon's Harvest*, 1921; *Collected Poems*, 1921; *The Man Who Died Twice*, 1924.

The most important critical writings on Mr. Robinson are by John Drinkwater in the *Yale Review*, XI (April, 1922), 467–76; by Amy Lowell in *Tendencies in Modern American Poetry*, pp. 3–75; and by Louis Untermeyer, in *The New Era in American Poetry*, pp. 111–35.

III

Robert Frost

I

THE temptation to generalize from Mr. Frost about art and artists is almost too strong to resist, even though there is no subject which so defies abstractions. It is doubtless wiser to write specifically about him, letting the generalizations take care of themselves; and it is beyond question appropriate to do so, because this is his own method in writing about life. He is persistently and cheerfully single-minded about what he wants life to yield him, but common-sensible and almost hard-headed too. To think of the poet who wrote for twenty years on an average literary income of ten dollars as stalking through the world with a somber eye fixed on achievement and fame would be quite to misconceive him. Various pulls have swerved him from the direct path. Until the public came to know him it was the need of daily bread. Since that time it has been the desire of publishers and college presidents to thrust it upon him under distracting circumstances. "They have made a very tempting offer," he said of his first college call. "All the work in three days of the week. But the trouble is that it takes me two days to unscrew, and two to screw up again." He has tried carrying scheduled duties, but now that daily bread can be secured by a little less sweat of brow than formerly, he reverts persistently to his old desire, which is to live relaxed and unhurried, not in indolence— for he likes to work with his hands—and not in solitude—for he is most companionable—but in such quiet circumstances that, as he has said, he can lean against life until it stings him into utterance.

The fact that his first three volumes—two of them quite slender—hold all that he cared to preserve from nearly a quarter of a century of writing, and that it was seven years before

419973

a fourth was added to them, shows how free
he is from either inward or outward pressure. He seems never to have been impatient
for a hearing, and never to have inclined
toward putting his own hopes or fears or
special convictions into print. He does not
plan poetic projects nor preach poetic dis-
quisitions on life. The infrequency of his
publishing has led to the comment that he is
not really a poet, but only a man who writes
poetry. The distinction is a valid one, but
the application to Mr. Frost should be
exactly transposed. It is only the journalistic versifiers—Walt Mason, Edgar Guest,
and the like—who can turn out copy every
day. It should be said of the poet what Mr.
Crothers said of the average citizen in his
Observations on Votes for Women, that he is
allowed time off occasionally to attend to his
daily affairs. Mr. Frost has taken his time,
yet, all things considered, it is a surprising
fact, for which a prominent publisher is
authority, that in point of American sales in
recent years, excluding the daily versifiers,
Masefield and Masters are the only two poets

who have surpassed Mr. Frost, the least prolific of contemporary writers.

II

As a so-called modern poet Mr. Frost is both old-fashioned and new-fashioned in his manner of writing. *A Boy's Will* is composed wholly in established lyric forms, in line, stanza, and rhyme usages. The two later volumes are more generally in an iambic pentameter which carries into effect his definite theory of versification.

In this connection everyone who is interested in modern prosody knows that until recently the theory of versification has been very much obscured by the efforts of critics to prove that every line which was supposed to conform to a certain measure actually did so. In an iambic measure an anapest has been an iambic with another label, and a trochee has been an iambic inverted. Pentameter has had either five stresses and ten syllables or an excuse for shortage or excess. The consequence has been that apologists have had about as much trouble with the conduct of

many of Shakespeare's lines as they have had
with the domestic vagaries of Henry VIII.
Their struggles have been amusing when
they came to such an incorrigible as

> Than the soft myrtle. But man, proud man.

Yet rather than surrender, they have forced
it into the strait-jacket of

> Te tum, te tum, te tum, te tum, te tum.

Within the last few years the discussion of
rhythm has grown to Cyclopean proportions.
(A bibliography of rhythm in the *American
Journal of Psychology*, 1913–18, has just been
characterized as "important but incom-
plete.") The one definite conclusion to be
drawn from all the discussion is that we
are probably on the way to a new and
sound science of verse. Such being the case, it
would be foolish and futile to dogmatize
just now on general principles; but it is still
reasonable to explain what a particular poet
believes about verse, and what he thinks he
is doing when he writes it.

Mr. Frost contends that there are two
rival factors in every verse product: the

absolute rhythm demanded by the adopted pattern, and the flexible rhythm demanded by the accents of the successive words and by the particular stresses needed among the words. The former is illustrated by the mechanical quatrain composed by Dr. Johnson to prove that rhyme and rhythm do not necessarily make poetry (and even in this there is one break from the pattern).

> I put my hat upon my head,
>   And walked into the Strand;
> And there I met another man,
>   Whose hat was in his hand.

The latter is illustrated by the doubts of a young actor in a play within a play who is given a single line for his part, and anxiously wanders about the stage debating whether to say,

> There is a *lady* outside, who desires an audience, or
> There is a lady *outside*, who desires an audience, or
> There *is* a lady outside, who desires an audience.

Says Mr. Frost, admitting these two rival factors, neither should be entirely subjected to the other. In what is called iambic pentameter, most of the feet should be iambic, and most of the lines should have five stresses; but in cases of departure from the pattern, there is nothing to explain away or condone; the rhythm will return to it. There is nothing new in this idea—except among prosodists. The poets have always acted on it. The opening lines of "Thanatopsis" or "The Princess" illustrate it, as does almost any spontaneous blank verse. In the conversational tone of his pentameters, Mr. Frost simply shows that he stands with less formal writers. See how the theory applies to "The Runaway," for example:

Once when the snow of the year was beginning to fall,
We stopped by a mountain pasture to say, "Whose colt?"

This is written on an iambic pentameter pattern, but, honestly scanned, the first line opens with four dactyls and the second ends with three stressed syllables in succession:

Once when the snow of the year was be- ginning to fall
We stopped by a moun- tain pas- ture to say "Whose colt?"

But he is not solicitous (as are W. B. Yeats or Vachel Lindsay, whose theory and practice are quite different from his). He says to let the spoken word and the verse pattern fight out the issue; and the best poetry results from the nicest compromise between them. So in the forms of all his poems there is a not too insistent design. This appears in rhyme, as well as in rhythm. In "The Runaway" at first glance the rhyme seems to be quite casual; but at second or third glance the twenty-one lines fall into three groups of six and seven and eight, each of which has a nice symmetry of rhyme scheme:

a b a c b c; a b c c a b c; a a b c c b d d.

However, in a brief discussion such as this, it is easy to place too much emphasis on questions of form, which, though sometimes interesting, are always subordinate in poetry. The main point to remember in connection with this aspect of Mr. Frost's work is that his effects are never accidental. His poems are his expression of a definite theory about poetic form.

III

In its broadest divisions Mr. Frost's work falls into lyrics and sketches—the records of moments of feeling and moments of observation. *A Boy's Will* is made up wholly of the first type, *North of Boston* and *Mountain Interval* largely of the second. The little songs in *A Boy's Will* tell by implication something of a poet's experience in deciding on what life owes him, and what he owes the world. The poet and his bride withdraw into the happy seclusion of the countryside, and here without ecstacizing or sentimentalizing over it they enjoy its quiet and peace and beauty. But they find that care cannot be wantonly thrust forth by happiness, and in the end they come down the hills and into the world again.

> Out through the fields and the woods
>   And over the walls I have wended.
> I have climbed the hills of view,
>   And looked at the world, and descended;
> I have come by the highway home,
>   And lo, it is ended.

Each of the songs was written for itself; they would not have been genuine, the poet has said, if they had been done to measure; and they can be read separately for their beauty. Yet the unity is there, as he discovered it and revealed it in his annotated Table of Contents, and they can be read together for their truth.

Except for the forewords and afterwords the later volumes contain few of these brief lyrics. They in turn, without being too mechanically grouped, may be separated into poems largely on men and women in the presence of nature, and poems largely on men and women in their relation to each other. "Mending Wall," "The Woodpile," and "The Mountain," are of the former sort. Two country neighbors meet each spring to repair the stone walls upset by winter frosts, spring thaws, and the hunters. One of them —the poet—speculates on the fact that every year nature overthrows man's artifice; the other sturdily labors to restore his own handiwork because "Good fences make good neighbors." It is all presented in simplest fashion, with no word of intruded comment or explanation. The pile of wood stands deserted and exposed out in the winter snows. One prop has fallen and vines have covered it in the years since it was laboriously stacked there. Where has the builder gone who stored the fuel that is now wasting "with the slow, smokeless burning of decay"? Again the mystery of nature, "rock-ribbed and ancient as the sun," and man, the transitory. Imagination lingers when the poem comes to an end. The Mountain spreads so wide that on its lower slopes and on the fringe of land around it there are only sixty voters in the township. It looms high in their midst, dominating and limiting life; few have time to go to the top, and fewer still, a surviving curiosity. There is a rigor in the earth north of Boston. Winter is insistent. It frightens the colt who is unused to snow, lets death descend on the autumn, breaks down the birches with its ice storms, overthrows the walls, and reluctantly succumbs to spring. Spring marks rather the departure of the ice king than the coming of plenty; and enjoyment of summer is delegated to the city vacationists.

So the characters presented by Mr. Frost are products of duress and adversity. They live in a country which has come to old age on arid tradition. They are unacquainted with mirth or song or play. Their human contacts have not been varied, for they are far from the main-traveled roads; and the summer visitors, who do not understand them, call them "natives" but think of them as peasants. With little to alleviate life, they have lost the traits of Pauline charity. Hard pride and grim endurance have lined their faces, labor has bowed their backs, and inbreeding has done the rest. They are, in short, the same people today whom Whittier characterized as being a hundred years ago:

> Church-goers, fearful of the unseen Powers,
> But grumbling over pulpit tax and pew-rent,
> Saving, as shrewd economists, their souls
> And winter pork, with the least possible outlay
> Of salt and sanctity; in daily life
> Showing as little actual comprehension
> Of Christian charity and love and duty
> As if the Sermon on the Mount had been
> Outdated like a last year's almanac.

Such people are not to be found only in New England. Similar conditions produce the same type anywhere in Anglo-Saxondom; but their characters are like their speech, which has the general features of the English tongue, with a local twang and idiom. And Mr. Frost has fixed them in his pictures.

IV

As a poet Mr. Frost is no more concerned with the world of affairs than Mr. Robinson is. He does not discuss institutions, movements, tendencies. He has no reforms to advocate, or theories to advance. He does not even propound a philosophy of life. On the whole, if we are to deduce one from his collected work, it is the philosophy that a cheerful, persistent man of hard-headed common sense might be expected to have. His convictions have not grown so much from what he has thought as from what he has felt; and because they are the fruit of his temperament rather than the children of his mind, he has very little to say about them—just takes them for granted. He feels that while this is not the best of all possible worlds, it is the best one that he knows, and that as far as his life in it is concerned it is pretty much a world of his own making. If he has misgivings at the actual ugliness of life he admits them and records them, but he is reassured by its actual and potential beauties. Of all that life has to give he finds nothing to rival sympathetic companionship —between neighbors, friends, parents and children, husbands and wives.

He has very seldom drawn open analogies from nature, or written openly about himself; but he has done both in the last stanza of "Birches," and it goes far toward explaining his reticent optimism:

So was I once myself a swinger of birches;
And so I dream of going back to be.
It's when I'm weary of considerations,
And life is too much like a pathless wood
Where your face burns and tickles with the cobwebs
Broken across it, and one eye is weeping
From a twig's having lashed across it open.
I'd like to get away from earth awhile
And then come back to it and begin over.
May no fate wilfully misunderstand me

And half grant what I wish and snatch me away
Not to return.   Earth's the right place for love:
I don't know where it's likely to go better.
I'd like to go by climbing a birch tree
And climb black branches up a snow-white trunk
Toward heaven, till the tree could bear no more,
But dipped its top and set me down again.
That would be good both going and coming back.
One could do worse than be a swinger of birches.

BIOGRAPHICAL NOTE

Robert Frost, descendant of New England through
many generations, was born in San Francisco in 1875.
After the death of his father, when he was ten years
old, he returned East with his mother to the Massachusetts mill town of Lawrence, where he graduated
from high school in 1892. At Dartmouth College the
next autumn and winter, and five years later at Harvard, although full of zeal as a student, he was like
most creative artists, ill-attuned to the fixed routines
and courses of study, persisting but a few months the
first time and but two years the second. In teaching,
for which he has a natural bent, he was original in
method and very successful, attracting the attention of
the New Hampshire superintendent of schools by his
work; but this routine, too, proved irksome, and for
eleven years, 1901–12, Mr. Frost combined farming
and authorship.   Yet the soil of the New Hampshire
farm and of the publishing world were equally sterile—

twenty years of poetry had yielded $200—and in the autumn of 1912 he sold the farm and went to England with his wife and children and a sheaf of manuscripts. Here, in a village not far from London, he settled happily, and one day, looking over his poems of long accumulation, he found in them—as he jotted down notes of their contents—a sequence that he had not planned in advance. This is the sequence indicated in the Table of Contents of *A Boy's Will*, published in London in 1913. Recognition came at once. *North of Boston* followed in the spring of 1914, and history repeated itself, as in the cases of Walt Whitman and Joaquin Miller, in the English recognition of an American poet who was unacknowledged at home. These two volumes were soon republished in New York, Mr. Frost returned with his household in 1915, and *Mountain Interval* appeared in 1916. The poet, however, has since that time re-proved his independence by refusing to let popularity hurry him into print, and no further volume appeared until 1923. It is interesting that formal education has not even yet surrendered claim to him. He was prevailed upon to teach in Amherst College from 1916 to 1919, and from 1923 on, and, in the interim, was persuaded to go to the University of Michigan, this time with no specified class duties. He was awarded the Pulitzer Prize for the best volume of American poetry published in 1923, his long-delayed fourth work, *New Hampshire*.

Robert Frost

Mr. Frost's publications are as follows: *A Boy's Will*, 1913; *North of Boston*, 1914; *Mountain Interval*, 1916; *New Hampshire*, 1923.

The best critical articles on his work are: G. R. Elliot, "The Neighborliness of Robert Frost," *Nation*, December 6, 1919; Edward Garnett, "Robert Frost—New American Poet," *Atlantic*, CXVI (August, 1915), 214-21; Amy Lowell, *Tendencies in Modern American Poetry*, pp. 79-136; Louis Untermeyer, *The New Era in American Poetry*, pp. 15-39.

IV

*The Voice of Chicago — Edgar Lee
Masters and Carl Sandburg*

I

WITH the years just following the
World's Fair of 1893, Chicago

> Gigantic, wilful, young, ...
> With restless violent hands and casual tongue

became vocal in a new way. The city had
never been voiceless, though up to these years
the rest of the country had heard little from
it but the shouts from the wheat pit and the
uproar of the Haymarket riots. Long after
Far West and Gulf and Tidewater and southern mountain regions had been heard from
in poetry and fiction, Chicago had not told
a story, written a song, or painted a picture. The school child—who is averagely
unschooled in contemporary literature—required to make a list of Illinois authors,

searches out the imported Eugene Field, adds Lincoln, if reminded that the great president wrote great prose, and stops at that.

The Columbian Exposition supplied an immense new impulse. Theodore Thomas and the orchestra, William M. R. French and the art museum, William R. Harper and the university, furnished rallying-points and attracted the support of local millions. Young authors, artists, sculptors, came to town and were patronized, not always for their own good, by the same wealth that unsettled individuals even while it was beneficently establishing institutions. Certain college students in the East, rebellious at the domination of the Victorians, and the passing generation of New Englanders, decided to "put Chicago on the map." Stone and Kimball started publishing. The *Chap Book* was founded. The *Dial* continued on its modest way. Orchestra, art museum, and university flourished, Moody and Masters came to town— and still the local Miltons were mute and inglorious. Yet something real had happened. It was in those days that literary

Chicago was born, and when it became of age—in about 1914—Mr. Masters' voice had changed, and he and Carl Sandburg and Sherwood Anderson and Floyd Dell and a dozen others began to speak so loud and clear that all the country has had to listen.

II

Mr. Masters' *Spoon River Anthology* (1915) in the first years after publication was altogether the most read and most talked-of volume of poetry that had ever been written in America. Coming out in instalments over a long period in a distinguished but obscure weekly, William Marion Reedy's *Mirror*, the collected poems are said to have been offered to several publishers before their final acceptance. Their circulation was rapid from the first. People who really knew poetry were interested and amused at their combination of a very old Greek form with the doings of an Illinois town. People who were allured but disappointed by the glitter and the hollowness of much of the new poetry were refreshed by the grim substance of this book.

People who had never read poetry before took up the volume because they heard it had "punch." Villagers read it to protest as later they were to protest at *Winesburg, Ohio,* and at *Main Street.* And the literary throng was swelled, of course, as all literary throngs always are, by the novelty hunters, and the "shocker" hunters, and the tasters who want at least a spoonful of what everybody is reading.

Out of all the chorus of comment that greeted it there were two most insistent notes—the same two that greeted *Leaves of Grass* sixty years earlier—that it was "queer," and that it was morbid. There was reason for both charges. The *Anthology* was different from most modern verse, though its novelty lay in its return to an old and accepted Greek form. It was also disturbing to the sensitive, for it acknowledged and expatiated on the presence of hypocrisy, hate, greed, and lust in village life. Some of the objectors denied that any such conditions existed, or at any rate that they were typical; others fell back on the contention that even if the poems were based on fact such facts had no place in art, or even in print. What almost everyone failed to see was that in Mr. Masters' mind, while these conditions needed acknowledgment, they were not the most important elements in the life of Spoon River; for he acknowledged also the presence of love, loyalty, spiritual strength, in the average town. And the people whom he admired and whom he massed toward the end of the collection, although not successful in material ways, were happy conquerors of circumstance.

It would be futile, however, to dodge or deny the fact that Mr. Masters dwells long, not only on love, but on passion and lust in *Spoon River* and in other volumes; and that he pays more circumstantial attention to the latter than many a seasoned and unprudish reader finds to his taste. But Mr. Masters' treatment of sex should not be regarded as unique. It is part of the history of contemporary literature. In a clearer perspective than we can now command the future historian will be able to show the change from the treatment of love between man and woman as something inspired by a stimulus from without to the present-day discussion of the same thing as springing from an impulse from within. It was the old fashion to present Launcelot and Guinevere as adorable persons and then to set them adoring at sight. It is the new mode to present them as smoldering and highly inflammable and to set them aflame at meeting. It was the old romantic assumption that neither could have loved any but the other. It is the modern view that either might have fallen in love with any equally eligible object of desire. The modern realist says:

"This is a disturbing thought only because it is a disturbing fact. If you don't like it, bring an indictment against life and not against art. Read Freud, Jung, Ellen Key, Havelock Ellis, and stop protesting at poetry, fiction, and drama. Sociology, philosophy, psychology, literature—they are all dealing with the same thing. As a matter of fact literature is nothing if not an index to the thought of the times."

If the protester can marshal his powers enough to reply that, even if this be true, he still wishes literature would not indicate so steadily the unhappy and desperate aspects of love, the realist rejoins:

"But there is nothing new in this attitude of art, except in the explicitness with which the subject is handled. Literature seldom deals with happiness; but regularly with the quest for it or the loss of it. How much placid happiness is there in the great love stories of the ages? Antigone? Penelope? Helen? Dido? Griselda? Guinevere? Francesca? Juliet? Why did the fairy tale always *end* with, 'And so they lived happily ever after'? Because uneventful happiness has no story to tell!"

The problem is a complicated and bewildering one—like life itself—better fitted for discussion in a whole volume than a few casual paragraphs. An ample treatment of it should include a dozen contributory, interweaving factors: the entrance into social consciousness of biological knowledge, the changing place of religion and the church, the woman's movement and the challenge to the old theory of the home, the discrediting of self-denial and the enthronement of self-expression, the allied theories of eugenics and birth control, the influence of the world-war—time and some future philosopher-historian will unravel the tangle. But in the meanwhile Mr. Masters is contributing to it by what he writes on the intimate matters of sex. Given the frankness of Whitman, the analytical gifts of Browning, and the bias of Freud, Mr. Masters was bound to write some of the passages that have startled some of his readers. The issue —if there be an issue—is not as to whether these passages are true to life, but partly as to whether the devious ways of love and the explicit experiences of passion have not been overstressed, and partly as to whether they are good substance for pure literature. The reader of Masters' "Victor Rafolski" or "The Widow La Rue" or Maugham's *The Moon and Sixpence* or Hergesheimer's *Cytherea* or the run of many other novels and poems is less likely to be disturbed by the joy of elevated thoughts than by the rousing of elevated pulse. Literature, like social philosophy, is becoming physiological, and glands are regulating personality on every printed page.

There is no use in protesting on ethical grounds that such stories ought not to be written. They will be written as long as people are thinking the things that are in them; but it is quite pertinent to ask whether the problems and the phenomena involved in such stories are not better adapted to an intellectual treatment in the essay than they are to an emotional one in poetry or fiction. For many of us Bernard Shaw proves that they are by the superiority of most of his prefaces to most of his plays; and it is enough for us to say of such narrative literature what Emerson once said of the communion service, that the end of our opposition is that we are not interested in it; that we are content that it shall go on to the end of time if it please God and please man. We may solve for ourselves the immediate problem as to whether it ought to be read by not reading it—if we can afford not to. And we shall do well to avoid the responsibility of setting up a general censorship.

III

However, neither the informality of style nor the grimness of subject-matter that characterized *Spoon River* are the overwhelming features of Mr. Masters' poetry as a whole. Mr. Reedy, the editor of the *Mirror*, actually persuaded him to give over an earlier conventional manner for the writing of his epitaphs. Some of the most applauded verses in *Songs and Satires* (1916) were reprinted from a volume of 1898 which was never put into general circulation. In the finished form of *Helen of Troy* and *When under the Icy Eaves*, Mr. Masters was minding his poetical *p*'s and *q*'s; a practice to which he returns at times in almost every later volume. And as far as subject-matter goes, of the thoughts that catch and hold his imagination there is none more insistent than the one that sets him again and again to inquiring into the mystery of things, and to trying—little as

the careless reader would suspect it—to sat-
isfy himself with Matthew Arnold's borrowed formula, that "reason and the will of
God prevail." Life, he says throughout his
writings, is an almost inextricable confusion.
In the experience of the individual and of the
group, influences and motives and actions
are in continual conflict. It is hard to tell
strength from weakness, honesty from dupli-
city, the ennobling from the debasing. But
there are such traits as strength and honesty
and nobility, and there is an all-embracing
design in human life. This is the theme of
"The Loom" in brief, and at length it is the
theme of *Domesday Book*, the closest contemporary parallel of Browning's manifold
story of Pompilia and Caponsacchi.

It is not the point of *Domesday Book* to
show the directness of God's ways so much
as to demonstrate the complex deviousness of
man's. Shortly after the close of the world-
war a young woman is found dead by a river-
side near an Illinois town. In this town an
educated man of independent means, impressed by the tragic wastefulness of life as

most people live it, has succeeded in becoming coroner, because of the chance it will give him to inquire into the unpublished facts of people's tragedies, and perhaps to find out the cause of the waste and to arrive at principles by which it can be avoided. He traces this girl's entire career in all relationships, and in the search follows the ripples which her actions have started until they reach individuals who seem insulated from her by time and space and every social barrier. Out of the social chaos this inquirer seeks order. In the single case before him he finds, of course, no general solution. He is neither successful nor defeated so far; but in the very fact of continued search his belief in the possibility of finding is made evident.

In this there is something of the old Greek tradition which saw man beset by his own character, but there is quite as much of the modern point of view which sees man beset by society. Spoon River, while just as broadly human as Mr. Robinson's Tilbury or Mr. Frost's grim countryside, is much more definitely touched by the tide of events. The generations there are still deeply affected by the memories of the Civil War; they remember Lincoln and Altgeld; they are conscious of Bryan and Roosevelt; they are involved in politics and in church and bank scandals; they buy and sell with one another, and have daily jobs. Mr. Masters' Chicago is an equally definite place with named streets and buildings, and offices in them where the dark doings of high finance and low politics are planned. It is a city from which the troops went forth to France full of heroic optimism, and to which some of them returned with hopes sadly shaken. Yet Chicago is a symbol, too. Seated at the foot of the Great Lakes and beside *The Great Valley* of the Mississippi, with an outlet *Toward the Gulf* and *The Open Sea* beyond, it presents a picture of a present full of sordidness and squalor, but it fronts a future and in the future a fine hope.

IV

I remember vividly the mixture of disgust and contempt with which an official in an old eastern public library handed me a copy of Carl Sandburg's *Chicago Poems* just after the publication in 1916. He resented having to include it in the American poetry section. When I read the opening line: "Hog Butcher for the World," I understood his feeling, and I also felt fairly certain that I had then read all that he ever had read or ever would read in the book. His manner made me feel guiltily responsible for the brutal city and the brutal line. Yet the objections raised by conservatives to the brutality of Mr. Sandburg's poems are quite as open to challenge as the strictures on the cynical pessimism of Edgar Lee Masters. The opening poem on Chicago is a glorification of muscular power honestly used.

Chicago is a tall, bold slugger set vividly against the little soft cities. It is no more than an elaboration of the lines from William Vaughn Moody quoted at the first of the chapter. The address "To a Contemporary Bunkshooter" is the challenge of a common man who is capable of vulgar talk himself though he resents vulgar treatment of sacred themes. So he sneers, "Where do you get that

stuff? . . . . Go ahead and bust all the chairs
you want to." Poetry has always shaken the
lance at shams and charlatans. The objection
is not to the poetic material, then, but to the
poetic manner which chooses to treat of a
brute subject in language that the subject
might use of himself or of another like him.
The issue is on the old question as to the
rival claims of elegant language and of common diction in literature; the question that
Dante and Chaucer and Wordsworth and
Whitman all settled in favor of the simpler
colloquial forms. When Mr. Sandburg writes
of "The Sins of Kalamazoo" he assails the
town in the choice language of "a loafer
lagging along"; and when he arraigns the
political thievery of the gangsters he does it
by letting a political thief say without
shame:

Nothin' ever sticks to my fingers, nah, nah, nothin'
   like that,
But there ain't no law we got to wear mittens—huh—
   is there?
Mittens, that's a good one—mittens!
There oughta be a law everybody wear mittens.

However, this is not the only diction that Mr. Sandburg uses. The second entry in *Chicago Poems* begins:

> The shadows of the ships
> Rock on the crest
> In the low blue lustre
> Of the soft inrolling tide.

Words are as naturally fitted to subject as they are in the vulgar but poetically suggestive phrasing of the vulgar subject of grafting. And the third poem in the same volume ends with:

> And then one day I got a true look at the Poor, millions of the Poor, patient and toiling; more patient than crags, tides and stars; innumerable, patient as the darkness of night—and all broken, humble ruins of nations.

It is a passage pervaded with the dignity of high respect for the sufferings of the oppressed. It is obvious that the poet does not sing one tune alone or in only one key; that at times he is simply speaking in character as any novelist or dramatist makes his characters do. He merely pays his readers the compliment of leaving out quotation marks.

Perhaps only those who have heard Carl Sandburg's voice in conversation, in ballad singing, and in the reading of his own poems can quite respond to his artistry, for it is a voice of melodious rhythms, full of depth and tenderness, quite free from vehemence, simply used without a touch of "elocution," but with a complete command of tone effects, and the nicest possible feeling for value of the retard and the half-pause. It is a voice for quiet ironies rather than for noisy invectives, and pre-eminently for the expression of sympathies rather than antipathies.

V

In the changing world of which Carl Sandburg finds himself a part and which he knows from the bottom up, he is aware, of course, of social injustice, and he makes his protest against it; but as one of the people himself he is not overwhelmed by the thought of social oppression, because he is upheld by the confidence that the future has better things in store:

When I, the People, learn to remember, when I the People, use the lessons of yesterday and no longer forget who robbed me last year, who played me for a fool—then there will be no speaker in all the world to say the name: "The People," with any fleck of a sneer in his voice or any far-off smile of derision.

It is the pathos rather than the tragedy of the mob that moves him. It is pathetic that toilers toil all day and all year with no prospect but toil and dirt and poverty; that the city takes the fresh gold of life poured into it and turns it to dross; that the fish-crier, and the little shopkeeper, and the immigrant laborer on a picnic with his family, with so little to rejoice in, still ascend the hills of happiness. But it is pathetic, too, that wealth in its temporary pride builds corporations and palaces and mausoleums and fences to fend off the poor, and persists in forgetting that at the end are cool tombs, and that nothing can fend off death and the rain and tomorrow.

When he escapes from the town he finds reassurance in the broader expanses of time and space:

O prairie mother, I am one of your boys. . . . .
I speak of new cities and new people,

I tell you the past is a bucket of ashes.
I tell you yesterday is a wind gone down,
    a sun dropped in the west,
I tell you there is nothing in the world,
    only an ocean of tomorrows;
    a sky of tomorrows.

The prairie nourishes the living and houses the dead, symbol of eternity. Across it lie the railroads, slender ribbons of steel connecting the transitory towns. Yet the careless take the towns more seriously than the great stretches between and the reaches of time beyond all living towns.

I am riding on a limited express, one of the crack trains
    of the nation.
Hurtling across the prairie into blue haze and dark air
    go fifteen all-steel coaches holding a thousand
    people.
(All the coaches shall be scrap and rust and all the men
    and women laughing in the diners and sleepers
    shall pass to ashes.)
I ask a man in the smoker where he is going and he
    answers: "Omaha."

So as a poet he lives in the midst of the great spaces, but as a poet, too, he lives in the presence of beauty, and he finds it on every side—in the manifold moods of earth and sky and sea, in the innocence of childhood, in honest love and honest labor, in homely ways and homely places.

> So it goes; there are accomplished facts.
> Ride, ride, ride on the great new blimps—
> Cross unheard-of oceans, circle the planet.
> When you come back we may sit by five holly-
> hocks.
> We might listen to boys fighting for marbles.
> The grasshopper will look good to us.
> So it goes. . . . .

Carl Sandburg treats life frankly because on the whole he likes it and believes in it. Men who dodge the issue of describing things as they see them are usually afraid to face the facts; but to him life with all its ugliness is touched with beauty and filled with solemnity. So in his individual way he sings the song of the people and of the days to come.

With Masters and Sandburg Chicago's tongue has ceased to be "casual."

Some Contemporary Americans

BIOGRAPHICAL NOTE

Edgar Lee Masters was born in Kansas in 1869, the birth year of Moody and Robinson. In early childhood he came to Illinois. As a student at Knox College he became keenly interested in the classics, but under parental pressure he entered the law, in which he has had a successful career. People who exclaim at the fact of a lawyer's suddenly becoming the most read poet in America do not know that Mr. Masters wrote poetry from boyhood, and that the forgotten volumes produced before the *Spoon River Anthology* of 1915 were as many in number as the rapidly appearing succession which since that year have contributed to his celebrity today.

His publications have been as follows: *A Book of Verses*, 1898; *Maximilian* (poetic drama), 1902; *The New Star Chambers and Other Essays*, 1904; *Blood of the Prophets*, 1905; *Althea* (a play), 1907; *The Trifler* (a play), 1908; *Spoon River Anthology*, 1915; *Songs and Satires*, 1916; *The Great Valley*, 1916; *Toward the Gulf*, 1918; *Starved Rock*, 1919; *Domesday Book*, 1920; *Mitch Miller* (a boy's story), 1920; *The Open Sea*, 1921; *Children of the Market Place* (a novel), 1922; *The Nuptial Flight*, 1923.

The most important critical articles are Joyce Kilmer, in the *Bookman*, November, 1916; Amy Lowell, *Tendencies in Modern American Poetry*, pp. 137–232; Louis Untermeyer, *The New Era in American Poetry*, pp. 161–88; W. H. Wright, in the *Forum*, January, 1916.

The Voice of Chicago

Carl Sandburg was born in Galesburg, Illinois, in 1878. During boyhood he came to know the working world through his varied jobs in unskilled labor. He served in the war with Spain in 1898, then went to Lombard College in his home town for three years, and again had a miscellany of jobs, though now as a brain worker. Since 1914, he has been on the staff of the *Chicago Daily News*. Like Mr. Masters, Mr. Sandburg felt his way toward poetry long before he gained a hearing. In 1914, ten years after the publication of his first booklet, his *Chicago* with a group of other poems won the $200 Levinson prize offered by *Poetry: A Magazine of Verse;* and in 1916 *Chicago Poems* appeared.

His publications have been as follows: *Chicago Poems*, 1916; *Cornhuskers*, 1918; *Smoke and Steel*, 1920; *Slabs of the Sunburnt West*, 1922; *Rootabaga Stories* (for children), 1922; *Rootabago Pigeons*, 1923.

The most important critical articles are: Amy Lowell, *Tendencies in Modern American Poetry*, pp. 137–232; P. Rosenfeld, in the *Bookman*, July, 1921; Louis Untermeyer, *The New Era in American Poetry*, pp. 95–111.

V

Amy Lowell

I

THE most energetic and unflagging experimenter, Miss Lowell's versatility became amazing. She has wielded a controversial cudgel with one hand, and, with the other she has written Chaucerian stanzas, polyphonic prose, monologues in her native New England dialect, irregular *vers libre*, conservative couplets, translations from the French, echoes from the Japanese, even primitive re-creations of Indian folk-lore." This, by one of her most friendly and admiring critics—who elsewhere calls her a "female Roosevelt among the Parnassians"—explains why Amy Lowell claims attention quite as much for her part in the experimental tendencies of the day as for her own intrinsic values; yet claims attention, it ought to be said emphatically, because, with all her zest for novelty, her work has more substance and less mere ingenuity than that of most of the conscious ultra-moderns.

At an age when Keats's and Shelley's careers were over, Miss Lowell decided to become a poet. For eight years she devoted herself to study, and at an age when Byron had died, she first published a poem. This is not stated by way of a jibe or a jest. It is unusual for any mature, intellectual person, not impelled by outward circumstances, to choose a career at twenty-eight, to work patiently in preparation until thirty-six, and to succeed. It is particularly unusual when the career is an artistic one; for the impulse toward art usually comes strong and early, and the schooling begins with childhood. Miss Lowell's step is not to be confused with the tardy recognition of a Hawthorne or a Browning, for each of them had one goal from youth; nor with the late beginning of a Richardson or a De Morgan, who strolled into authorship casually and had no theory about it. It suggests rather the experience of thousands of twentieth-century women, who have demanded for themselves something more than "days of strenuous idleness" and dependency on father, husband, dividend, or unearned increment. Or, if it seems gratuitous to identify a woman poet with the "Woman's Movement," it suggests the deferred choice of a profession by such good neighbors of Miss Lowell as William James or Henry L. Higginson, both of whom were quite as slow to decide as she.

It is beside the point to inquire into, or to speculate about, Miss Lowell's reasons for espousing poetry; but it is fair and proper to consider the results of so late a choice. It raises the question between the "poets are born" theory and the "genius and hard work" contention. In so many cases poets who were precocious from the start were also the hardest of hard workers that one can only guess as to the rival claims of endowment and training. But in this case, where free will evidently played so much more of a part than foreordination, there is a better chance of arriving at some conclusions.

II

It is a normal sequence in literary history that authors first fall into the fashions of the day, and afterward pay less attention to form as they develop greater depth, weight, and compactness of thought. Miss Lowell seems to have come toward writing with the usual deference for form; but coming at a time when there was an unusual stir in the air as to modes and manners of expression in all the arts, she seems never—or not yet— to have graduated from this youthful phase. She has developed into a theorist who occasionally writes poetry, and often what is a little less than poetry, rather than into an indubitable poet like Mr. Robinson or Mr. Frost. Yet in this she is not alone, for she has joined something which for want of a better term may be called a movement, and she is always audible toward the forefront of it.

Her first volume, *A Dome of Many-coloured Glass* (1912), was no more than one might have expected from an averagely gifted and studious, but more than averagely persistent, follower of the muse. The form was tight and the matter was tame. The influence of Tennyson was traceable and that of Keats was very strong. Much of it sounded like Emily Dickinson. The longest number was on the Athenaeum Library, where a large part of the preceding years had been passed. It included speculations on the nature of poetry, a little picture likening the poet to a diver poised for the plunge into a pool of mysterious new experience, and a fragment comparing him to a worker in stained glass— that most painstaking and unimpassioned of craftsmen. If Miss Lowell had been content to keep on in this vein, publishers and public would probably have been content to ignore her after another volume.

However, with *Sword Blades and Poppy Seed* (1914), she joined forces with the experimenters. This was the year when Ezra Pound issued a collection of Imagist poems, just before bidding farewell to the school, and the year before Miss Lowell was to avow herself as one of them and to stimulate the publishing of their three annual volumes of

1915, 1916, and 1917. Naturally, then, there were some examples of this type in *Sword Blades*. They and their kind have been much overdiscussed, and in spite of the fact that the Imagists themselves declared their principles to be "the essentials of all great poetry," their six tenets have been eyed askance as though they were strangely new. They are well enough as far as they go, but they fail to include all poetry, and much of the greatest, at the same time that they do include a great deal of what has long been regarded as no more than eloquent prose.[1] Here are two chill, night pictures, both in good Imagist style:

> And while the moon
> Swings low across the sky,
> Athwart a waving pine tree,
> And soon
> Tips all the needles there
> With silver sparkles, bitterly
> He gazes. . . . .

[1] See the good-humored essay on George Meredith, entitled, "An Unacknowledged Imagist," by John L. Lowes, in the *Nation*, February 24, 1916.

> While the earth has slumbered,
> All the air has been alive
> With feathery flakes descending,
> As if some northern Ceres reigned,
> Showering her silvery grain
> Over all the fields.

Each is marked by (1) common diction exactly used (although "athwart" is not the commonest of speech), (2) by varied rhythms, (3) by freedom in choice of subject, (4) by images, (5) by hard and clear effects, and (6) by concentration. One was published as verse by Miss Lowell in 1914, the other as prose by Thoreau in *Walden*, 1854.

These Imagist poems were in free verse, but that was a novelty that was no novelty, for Whitman's *Leaves of Grass* appeared only the next year after *Walden*.

A third experiment in style, used exclusively in *Can Grande's Castle* (1918), and supposed to be in quite a new set of harmonies, is described by one critic as "the first appearance in English of 'polyphonic prose'"; and he goes on to quote Miss Lowell's explanation:

Amy Lowell

"Polyphonic" means "many voiced," and the form is so-called because it makes use of all the "voices" of poetry, namely: meter, *vers libre*, assonance, alliteration, rhyme and return. It employs every form of rhythm, even prose rhythm, at times.

This is so "hard and clear" and dogmatic that it seems alluringly conclusive; yet all the elements, unless there be some doubt about "return," which Miss Lowell does not define, are to be found in the following passage by Whitman of 1855: I print it in block paragraph as polyphonic prose is printed:

The negro holds firmly the reins of his four horses —the block swags underneath on its tied-over chain; the negro that drives the dray of the stone-yard— sturdy and tall he stands, poised on one leg on the string piece; his blue shirt exposes his ample neck and breast, and loosens over his hip-band; his glance is calm and commanding—he tosses the slouch of his hat away from his forehead; the sun falls on his crispy hair and moustache—falls on the black of his perfect and polished limbs.

This speaks clearly enough in the six voices. *Meter:* "Sturdy and tall he stands, poised on one leg on the string piece," a perfect dactyllic hexameter; *vers libre:* the rest of the

passage; *assonance:* negro—holds, four—
horses, blue—loosens, etc.; *alliteration:* firmly
—four, drives—dray, sturdy—stands, etc.;
rhyme: reins—chain, stands—band, etc.; *return:*
falls—falls. Compare it with the following
from Miss Lowell's "Spring Day," the poem
in *Men, Women, and Ghosts* which begins with
the much discussed "Bath":

> Swirl of crowded streets. Shock and recoil of
> traffic. The stock-still brick façade of an old church,
> against which the waves of people lurch and with-
> draw. Flare of sunshine down side-streets. Eddies of
> light in the windows of chemists' shops, with their
> blue, gold, purple jars, darting colours far into the
> crowd. Loud bangs and tremors, murmurings out of
> high windows, whirring of machine belts, blurring
> of horses and motors. A quick spin and shudder of
> brakes on an electric car, and the jar of a church-bell
> knocking against the metal blue of the sky. I am a
> piece of the town, a bit of blown dust, thrust along
> with the crowd.

There are two main differences: One that the
passage from Whitman's "The Song of Myself" is not characteristic of the whole poem;
he wrote in this fashion at times, and at
times resorted to various other fashions.

The other is that the accumulation of devices is not so obvious and calculated in Whitman.

Polyphonic prose is immensely self-conscious; in Miss Lowell's hands all the effects are evidently calculated—as flagrantly so as in the artificial compositions classified as "program music." There is beyond doubt a clear relation between spoken and musical sounds and emotions or even objects, but it is a relation that may easily be forced too far. "Till Eulenspiegel" may have stimulated Strauss to a mischievous bit of music, but it becomes simply a joke by the time the hearer attempts to decide whether a certain jangle is meant to suggest a tin can tied to a cat's tail or a disturbance in the scullery. In word-music, where the meaning is made clear to begin with, the danger of disturbing the balance is all the greater. The reader of polyphonic prose is assaulted by decorative effects as brutally as a patron is in the lobby of a metropolitan hotel, where the adornment is so lavish and obtrusive that it eclipses the main design. Polyphonism as a distinct form of writing has made less of a ripple than Imagism; both are already lisping into silence on the shores of oblivion. Miss Lowell's experiments in poetic form have gone no farther, coming fortunately to an end before they reached the absurd extremes of Kreymborg, Arensburg, Cannell, and the rest of the *Others* as they described themselves in their joint volume of 1917.

Form, however, still pre-empts Miss Lowell's interest. Of late Chinese and Japanese poetry have incidentally come to the fore in her repertory; but the significant fact is that her allusions to the poet and to herself as a poet are always to a very self-conscious craftsman who is continually sitting down to think what she shall write instead of to write what she has thought.

> The cat and I
> Together on this sultry night
> Waited.
> He greatly desired a mouse,
> I, an idea.
> Neither ambition was gratified.

This inevitably suggests that if a luckless idea had strayed that way, the poet would have pounced on it and forthwith worried it to death. It is not the way that lasting poetry is achieved. It does not so much remind one of her favorite poet, Keats, as it does of Pope, spending a summer at Twickenham polishing the life out of a sonnet.

III

However, no one but the most deep-dyed technician can dwell indefinitely on an artist's manner of working. The more important questions are: What kind of mind and will and feeling are at work expressing themselves in this art? Has the artist anything to express? If so, what is it, and what is its value? How far do the mind and will and feeling of any body of readers respond to it? Miss Lowell has sounded a warning in her lines "On a Certain Critic" who wrote things about John Keats:

I wish you were here to damn him
With a good, round, agreeable oath,
    John Keats,
But just snap your fingers,
You and the moon will still love,
When he and his papers have slithered away
In the bodies of innumerable worms.

Still if one will read poets one must have opinions about them, and must express them in the face of possible deep damnation, even the chance of being blasted as "a sprig little gentleman . . . . with mincing fingers."

The poems in these volumes are crowded with sense impressions, color, sound, odor, and touch. They are seldom of the delicate or subtler kind or about majestic or expansive subjects. Only the moon appears in the large, and the cool radiance of Diana is a signal for the upspringing of emotions that have been repressed by day. For the most part the pictures, and every poem is built around one or more, are of limited and sophisticated subjects, gardens, studios, bookshops, museums, streets, each an accumulation of vivid and vividly stimulating objects that assail eye, ear, and nostril. The gamut of emotions is very limited. Skepticism banishes reverence and patriotic zest; there is no fear, nor hate, nor gaiety; and in the realm of love there is, with the rarest exceptions, only the love that is directly interfused with passion. This is an experience of yearnings and desires unsatisfied or of passion fulfilled. In many cases the lyrics are written as if by the man-lover who is dazzled by the beauty of his mistress, ravished by the thought of what her costume conceals and her continence withholds. The same restlessness prevails here as in her supervision of the garden or in her efforts at conjuring up a poem. There is energy on every page, but it is the energy of fidgets rather than of power.

Behind and beneath Miss Lowell's interest in freshness and independence of style and subject-matter is a foundation of old-fashioned literary formalism. In the years of her study she delved in literary tradition and accepted it. Literature was a matter of pictures, images, fleeting emotions caught in suggestive allusion. Sometimes it was keen and incisive as sword blades, sometimes soothing as poppy seed, but always it was something to be stored away in museums or shelved in libraries. Literature belonged to "the republic of letters," that most select of aristocracies, and never to the people on the streets. The populace appeared in it only as in the plays of Shakespeare, for effects of background and contrast; and in this literature, as in the plays of Shakespeare, there was no society, in the sense of social forces at work, but only people, for better or for worse. Moreover, this literature was cast in deftly conventional forms.

If Miss Lowell had been docile and acquiescent she might have contented herself with this compound of literary conventions to the end of the chapter. If she had enjoyed the serene independence of Robinson or Frost she might have gone on her way without expressed dissent from or disregard of literary tradition. If she had had the strongly liberal social convictions of Masters or Sandburg she might have joined the chorus of protest at the ways of the world. Instead she enlisted in the insurgent movement within the republic of letters. There was a select and widening circle ready to read, and especially ready to discuss, the sort of thing she undertook to write. The same influences that set her to work had prepared her public for her. Yet occasionally the real fervor of creation has arisen in her. "Patterns," "Guns as Keys," "The Dinner Party," "The Bronze Horses," "Lilacs," suggest power and passion that result in the poet's completely forgetting technique; not abandoning it, but using it surely and instinctively. These represent her finest moments.

On the whole, though, in this innocuous revolt, Miss Lowell is a kind of drum major. One cannot see the procession without seeing her, or admiring the skill with which she swings the baton. But when the parade is past, one can easily forget her until the trumpets blare again. She leads the way effectively, and one is glad to have her do it —glad that there are those who enjoy being drum majors. Then one pays farewell to her in the words with which she salutes Ezra Pound in her verses called "Astigmatism":

> Peace be with you [Sister],
> You have chosen your part.

Some Contemporary Americans

BIOGRAPHICAL NOTE

Miss Lowell was born in Brookline, Massachusetts, in 1874, coming from distinguished stock which included earliest New England pioneers, a minister to England, an eminent poet and publicist, and—in the person of her brother—a president of Harvard University. Her education was gained largely through tutoring and travel, the latter carrying her beyond the ordinary tourist points to Greece, Turkey, and Egypt. Although always interested in literature, she did not elect to become a poet until 1902. There followed eight years of study, the first publication of a poem in 1911, and of a volume in 1912. In the last ten years her output of poetry has been steady in volume and varied in kind, and has been supplemented by two books of criticism.

Miss Lowell's works are as follows: *A Dome of Many-coloured Glass*, 1912; *Sword Blades and Poppy Seed*, 1914; *Six French Poets*, 1915; *Men, Women and Ghosts*, 1916; *Tendencies in Modern American Poetry*, 1917; *Can Grande's Castle*, 1918; *Pictures of the Floating World*, 1919; *Legends*, 1921; *Fir-Flower Tablets; Translations from the Chinese* (with Florence Ayscough), 1921.

The best articles in criticism are by W. L. Phelps in "The Advance of English Poetry" in the *Twentieth Century*, pp. 245–56; Louis Untermeyer in *The New Era in American Poetry*, pp. 137–59; and Conrad Aiken, the *Dial*, November 2, 1918, and October 18, 1919.

VI

Edith Wharton

I

WITH the death of William Dean Howells in 1920, Mrs. Wharton was left as the connecting medium in American fiction between his generation and ours.[1] She is not a writer to stir enthusiasms, but she wins her full share of respectful admiration, as a distinguished representative of the old school is certain to do. One could begin to define current tend-

---

[1] For an approach to the whole question of contemporary fiction the following books are useful: General discussions: Sir Walter Besant, *The Art of Fiction*, 1884; Hamlin Garland, *Crumbling Idols*, 1894; W. D. Howells, *Criticism and Fiction*, 1895; and *Heroines of Fiction*, 1901; Henry James, "The Art of Fiction" (in *Partial Portraits*, 1888); Brander Matthews, *Aspects of Fiction*, 1896; and *The Historical Novel and Other Essays*, 1901; Frank Norris, *The Responsibilities of the Novelist*, 1901; Bliss Perry, *A Study of Prose Fiction*, 1902. Specific criticism: W. L. Phelps, *The Advance of the English Novel*, 1919; Carl Van Doren, *The American Novel*, 1921; and *Contemporary American Novelists*, 1922; H. Wilkinson, *Social Thought in American Fiction*, 1919.

encies among American novelists by saying that they reveal influences by which she was untouched. To many of the most fundamental changes in her lifetime Mrs. Wharton has been as oblivious as some who have been able to resist every outward influence. Yet she has been responsive to many; and to one, the breaking-down of America's cultural isolation, she has been a constant witness. When she began to write, her country had passed through a succession of moods, from the first excited resolve to be freed from English tradition, past a period of Anglophobia, to a state of artistic and intellectual indifference. It is enough to say of real values that the country as a whole regarded Emerson and Thoreau as amiable eccentrics and Whitman as a dangerous one, and of superficial values that in Mrs. Wharton's childhood Europe was being so freshly rediscovered to the American public that the fortunate few who were able to travel were the sort of innocents abroad who evoked Mark Twain's half-wrathful, half-scornful protests. In those same childhood years, too, American novel-readers were like American travelers. They were few in number, and if they read or if they traveled they turned their eyes toward the other side of the Atlantic.

In 1862, the year Mrs. Wharton was born, Cooper and Poe were dead, and Hawthorne and Mrs. Stowe, whose best work was done, were the only American story-tellers to set against Dickens and Thackeray, Bulwer and Collins, Reade and Trollope, and a half-dozen more whose novels were issued serially in American magazines or were scrambled through the press in pirated editions by competing American publishers. While Mrs. Wharton was being educated at home and abroad the tide turned. Twain, Harte, Cable, Harris, Craddock, started the output of stories on local types, circumstances, and traditions, and Howells and James went a step farther to develop the deep-seated differences between the children of the New World and the heirs to the Old World civilization. In this widespread expression of national self-consciousness it was natural for Mrs. Wharton to adopt the point of view and the manner of the latter two, and particularly of Henry James.

It was the habit of Howells and James to measure American character by what they knew of Europe. The results were informing to most Americans who thought that the average American was the norm of the universe; and it was a source of qualified pleasure to the few who feared that every difference from the Old World was a proof of inferiority in the new. James was fascinated by the evidence that all the people he met in London were consciously connected with a rich and varied social background—that they had what he called references. "A reference was then, to my mind" he wrote, "whether in a person or an object, the most becoming ornament possible." Introduced to the inner circle in Rome and in London, he made it his ambition "to establish connections with a world in which everything so bristled with connections"; and he tells with what joy he found himself, on the occasion of his first visit to George Eliot, running for the doctor in her service, since thereby, "a relation had

been dramatically determined." So, wherever his stories were located, he wrote always
with England and the Continent in the back
of his mind, whether he was presenting the
Englishman's or European's deference to tradition or the varying degrees of the American's obliviousness to it.

II

Mrs. Wharton had enjoyed the broaden-
ing influences of a bringing-up on both sides
of the Atlantic. She was particularly conscious of Italy, the resort of literary England
from Byron and Shelley and Keats to the
Brownings and George Eliot, to Hawthorne
and the Howells of *A Foregone Conclusion* and
the James of *Roderick Hudson*. Three of her
first eight books were located there—*The
Valley of Decision, Italian Gardens*, and *Italian
Backgrounds*—and all three were wholly
American in tone. The Englishman going
to Italy moves from one set of traditions to
another; the American, from no traditions to
a bewildering array of collections and recollections. The English gentleman in Italy is

tolerantly conscious of the difference between the code of his class and that of the corresponding class abroad; the American is reminded of the difference between breeding abroad and the general lack of breeding at home. Mrs. Wharton in her earliest books was no less conscious of this than most of her fellow-countrymen have been, with a consciousness which is betrayed in the amiable affectations of so late a book as *The Reef*, which introduces its hero on the way to a "luggage van" and ends by sending its heroine upstairs on a "lift."

Mrs. Wharton's education could not have been so cosmopolitan in effect if she had not belonged to the privileged class into which James was born and Howells naturally gravitated. This class composed her world. If she was to write at all, unless she deliberately went out of her way to collect material, they were her destined subject-matter. As a group, Mrs. Wharton's characters would be puzzled to know why the Lord's Prayer should include such a homely clause as "Give us this day our daily bread." Except for an occasional rather vulgar exploiter or an occasional decayed aristocrat, they all have incomes which proceed from invisible sources. The men, not infrequently, disappear into a vague realm of business, but the business is no more real than the sheep-herding of the shepherds and shepherdesses in the Latin pastorals. The world of labor is mentioned in but one of the novels, and in this for the sole purpose of supplying an added ground for a marital misunderstanding. These people, moreover, are not interested in social institutions of any kind. They ignore the marketplace no more than the bench and the bar, the church and the school; and no more so (except for a chapter or two in *The Age of Innocence*) than the whole world of institutionalized art—the theater, the opera-house, the art gallery, and the library. To be sure, they dissent from the crowd at every turn, but that is because of their instinctive feeling not so much that they themselves are right, as that the crowd is certain to be vulgarly wrong. They are full of refinements, and vigilantly aware of the dictates of propriety which make them live in continual fear of one another's faint disapproval, faintly but damningly expressed.

III

After writing of this world for twenty years, Mrs. Wharton has done best of all with it in one of her latest books, *The Age of Innocence*. It is a novel about the early seventies in New York, contrasting the rigid complacency of the old-school generation with the Bohemianism of the outer world of arts and letters, with the startling encroachments of the vulgar rich, with the dry rot among the elect of some who only pretended to concur— and whom, on account of their family status, the conservators of respectability pretended not to detect—and with the honestly decent, who were half-smothered by the unventilation of the exclusive New York dining-room and drawing-room.

The story centers around Newland Archer, an educated gentleman, his wife, born Edith Welland, and the Countess Ellen Olenska. Archer is a normal man who wishes the right to some little spontaneity of thought and expression. He marries a lovely girl, product of her narrow society, and therefore incapable of spontaneous feeling or flexible sympathies. He knows even before marriage that she is all this, but he discovers it just too late to make a decent withdrawal. His discovery comes from growing acquaintance with Countess Olenska, a well-born New Yorker, who has married a European scamp, and has been forced to leave him. She longs for the protection of respectable surroundings and friends, but after years of living in Europe she has lost the arts of suppression and evasion, which are needed for the social game of hide-and-go-seek as it is played in respectable society. Archer and the Countess love each other devotedly, but she gives him up on account of her respect for his wife, who is honest and dependent and a product of the conditions which have made her the limited thing she is. Each in her way is a victim of Mrs. Grundy—Edith Archer because she has never been allowed to grow up, and the Countess because, having grown up,

Mrs. Grundy would not tolerate her. The cosmopolitan woman, strong enough to have tilted with the code of the country if only herself had been involved, is balanced enough to give way before the just claims of the provincial wife.

The dominance of Mrs. Grundy all the way from a western mining town to a French chateau is the theme again of *The Custom of the Country*. Undine Spragg is first married and divorced from one Elmer Moffatt in Rocky Mountain Apex. Brought to New York when her father has made his pile, she is introduced to society, makes her way on the strength of her brilliant good looks, and is married to and divorced from a gentleman with a small patrimony, no business gifts, and an unrealized ambition for authorship. Then, as a result of much foreign residence, she annexes Raymond de Chelles, a Frenchman with a conservative family very like that of the heroine of James's *The American*. From him she runs away finally to remarry Moffatt, who throughout the story—but not conspicuously enough to stir the suspicions of the reader—has been her familiar spirit, subtly revealing his intimacy of feeling, and increasing his hold as his rise in financial circles parallels her meteoric ascent in the social world. Yet she never successfully defies the code, west, east, or across the sea. At the end with Moffatt and all his immense wealth, she is still confronted by the "custom of the country." Because of her divorce, "she could never be an ambassador's wife; and as she advanced to welcome her first guests she said to herself that it was the one part she was really made for."

Whenever Mrs. Wharton is writing of this limited polite society she writes in terms of the code and its domination over strong and weak alike; but outside the social pale she invokes forces of fate. In *Ethan Frome*, the grim story of Starkfield, Massachusetts, in which she demonstrates that she can work with undiluted American material, Ethan and Mattie meet their nemesis, not in any visitation from the outer world, but in dependency on the woman who has thwarted both their lives, and in lifelong confinement under the same isolated roof with her. What happens to Charity Royall in *Summer* we are not told; it stops where *The Scarlet Letter* begins; but we know that after her return to her home feeling "ashamed and yet secure," shame and security must have been her familiar spirits to the end.

Mrs. Wharton is like Henry James in trying to treat the polite hair-splitters of the drawing-room with respect, but she shares his covert contempt for the pallid grayness of their characters. Her really vital people are the ones whom her socially elect would with one voice describe as "impossible." James Huneker, commenting with gusto on *The House of Mirth*, and speculating as to whether it might be converted into a play, hit the point when he wrote to a friend:

Much of Lily Bart would evaporate in the hard, dry atmosphere of the theater, but that Jew Rosedale—he would loom up magnificently. I am not sure but that he would be the central figure in the play. He is wonderful. Studied from life, and yet a summing up of racial traits and tribal ambitions. He is much more vital and convincing than Selden, who, at the close, is a pale prig.

Edith Wharton

In all these stories, and in all her other stories, though Mrs. Wharton has no ethical thesis to present, she leaves no doubt as to her ethical convictions. Taken by and large, man is surrounded by forces quite beyond his own powers to control or defy. If he is a little man in a little world, little forces can intimidate him; if he is a more primitive creature in a more natural world, forces as relentless as the elements can crush him. The most triumphant of human powers is therefore not the defiance of fate, but the control of self. Lily Bart, the unheroic heroine of *The House of Mirth*, left impoverished on the death of her father, and compromising reluctantly with her moneyed ambition, defeats herself by delay and equivocation in a declining series of "affairs." A natural result of having low and sordid standards, but not enough genuine honesty to avow and pursue them, is that she succumbs to the circumstances that created her, and arrives at a miserable end. Ethan and Mattie, in their pitiful flight from circumstance, are caught and brought back to the life-sentence which is worse than capital punishment. But the Countess Olenska, unable to play the game according to Knickerbocker rules, resigns rather than violate them. Lawyer Royall, an apparent failure, instead of declining into bitterness, rises to fine heights of magnanimity when put to the hardest test of all; and in instance after instance spiritual success or failure is made to depend on spiritual integrity. Mrs. Wharton believes in the respectability that is grounded on honest self-respect.

IV

Mrs. Wharton is dispassionately intellectual. Only at the rarest intervals does an emotion sweep down the length of a page. Almost always, as in the fashion of Henry James, she is absorbed more in the lights and shades of analysis that precede and follow a climax than she is in the climax itself. She admires forthright people with a kind of speculative wonder. She is like Mr. Darrow of *The Reef*, who, as he followed the "massive movements and equally substantial utterances" of Miss Adelaide Painter, "was aware that, in a more detached frame of mind, he would have found an extreme interest in studying and classifying her," but who even at the moment felt in her "the absence of any of these unspoken perceptions which give significance to the most commonplace utterances." Her work as a whole is therefore characterized by keenness, brilliancy, or what we might call cleverness if we could forget the sophomoric turn which cleverness has taken in the last decade. Her cleverness is of the rather disconcerting sort that belongs to the social dictator who has a highly developed sense of form, a keen eye, and a keener tongue.

Everything offers a chance for a *mot*. A lover making calls with his betrothed on her family, after they had "rolled from one tribal doorstep to another," went home "with the feeling that he had been shown off like a wild animal cunningly trapped." A gentleman who was "a register of most of the scandals" in fifty years of New York society "was fully aware that his reputation for discretion increased his opportunities of

finding out what he wanted to know." A
stout dowager looked out on the world from
behind "the immense accretion of flesh which
had descended on her in middle life like a
flood of lava on a doomed city." A woman's
club type was "one of the ladies who pursue
Culture in bands, as though it were dangerous to meet alone."

The dialogue gleams and glimmers, seldom falling to the level on which even the
most vivacious actually talk. The speakers
measure every syllable, avoid direct statement, deal in devious implications. A man
is calling on an old intimate just after his
engagement has been announced to another,
and we suspect, younger woman. He enters.

"You?" she exclaimed; and the book she held
slipped from her hand. It was crude, certainly; unless
it were a touch of the finest art. The difficulty of classifying it disturbed Thursdale's balance.

"Why not?" he said, restoring the book. "Isn't
it my hour?" And as she made no answer, he added
gently, "Unless it's someone else's?"

She laid the book aside and sank back into her
chair. "Mine, merely," she said.

"I hope that doesn't mean that you're unwilling
to share it?"

"With you? By no means. You're welcome to my last crust."

He looked at her reproachfully. "Do you call this the last?"

She smiled as he dropped into the seat across the hearth. "It's a way of giving it more flavour."

He returned the smile. "A visit to you doesn't need such condiments."

She took this with just the right measure of retrospective amusement.

It is attenuated like the people whom it characterizes. It is doubtless quite fair to them. It has a distinction as they have and as their descriptions have. They are part of America today. God made them, therefore let them pass for men and women; but we can take them only as Mrs. Vervain took Thursdale, with just the right measure of retrospective amusement. They have the flavor of a scientific paper on "Modern Theories of Phosphorescence." If we cannot have lightning, but yearn at least for a moderate amount of direct sunlight, we must turn to other and younger Americans who are no longer content to occupy themselves with the pale reflections of European culture.

Some Contemporary Americans

BIOGRAPHICAL NOTE

Edith (Newbold Jones) Wharton was born in New York in 1862, a Daughter in fact, whether or not she is in membership, of the American Revolution. Bred as she was in the age of innocence of Victorian New York, she was not sent to schools, but learned with tutors, part of the time while in travel or foreign residence. To this she owes her acquaintance with French, Italian, and German languages and literatures. In 1885 she was married and went to live in Boston. Four years later her authorship began, or perhaps better, her publishing, with the appearance of both poems and short stories in *Scribner's Magazine*. In these and in her first novel, *The Touchstone*, the influence of Henry James was apparent. Since 1900, like Mr. James, she has divided her attention between the American scene and foreign backgrounds, and her energy between interpreting men and women in fiction and in the essay.

Mrs. Wharton's publications are as follows (the novels marked with *): *The Greater Inclination*, 1899; *The Touchstone*, 1900; *Crucial Instances*, 1901; *The Valley of Decision*, 1902; *Sanctuary*, 1903; *The Descent of Man and Other Stories*, 1904; *Italian Villas and Their Gardens*, 1904; *Italian Backgrounds*, 1905; *The House of Mirth*, 1905; *Madame de Treymes*, 1907; *The Fruit of the Tree*, 1907; *The Hermit and the Wild Woman*, 1908; *A Motor Flight through France*, 1908; *Artemis to Actaeon*, 1909; *Tales of Men and Ghosts*, 1910; *Ethan Frome*, 1911;

Edith Wharton

The Reef, 1912; *The Custom of the Country*, 1913; *Fighting France*, 1915; *Xingu and Other Stories*, 1916; *Summer*, 1917; *The Marne*, 1918; *In Morocco*, 1920; *French Ways and Their Meaning*, 1920; *The Age of Innocence*, 1920; *Glimpses of the Moon*, 1922; *A Son at the Front*, 1923.

The most important critical writings on Mrs. Wharton are: Edwin Bjorkman, *Voices of Tomorrow*, pp. 290–305; Carl Van Doren, *Contemporary American Novelists*, pp. 95–104; Francis Hackett, in the *New Republic* (February 10, 1917), pp. 50–52; Henry D. Sedgwick, *The New American Type*, pp. 51–97.

VII

Booth Tarkington

I

IN THE year 1916 the editor of one of the popular American monthly magazines, answering a telephone call, was startled a little to be asked how he would like "a half-dozen Tarkingtons." He expressed his interest and said to send them along. But they were not yet written. This would have been a poser for an editor of an old and conservative periodical; but the editor in question was a good business man, and as modern business is built on the reputation of the producer and the credit of the buyer, he agreed to take the half-dozen within the next year, and promised the manuscript-broker a sum that would be a respectable salary for a bank president. The stories came along, the circulation of the magazine rose steadily with them, and in the end a seventh contribution was secured at a 10 per cent increase in price. It turned out to be a very satisfactory arrangement for editor, broker, author, and reading-public. This does not prove very much; but it proves at least that by 1916 the author of *Monsieur Beaucaire* and *The Vanrevels*, *The Conquest of Canaan* and *The Turmoil*, *Penrod*, and *Seventeen* had established his market—that he had in him the elements of popularity; a fact which is not to be sniffed at. This was not to be all, however.

In 1920 Mr. Tarkington was awarded the Pulitzer prize for the best work of American fiction published in the preceding year, *The Magnificent Ambersons*, and in 1922 the same honor was conferred on him for *Alice Adams* of 1921. This, again, is no proof of immortality. No judges' award can usurp the verdict of popular consent and the lapse of time. Yet laurels twice offered by competent juries do at least carry with them the presumption that the recipient has in him some of the elements of excellence. There is no necessary relationship between excellence and contemporary popularity; but neither is there—as the cynic likes to insist—any inevitable divorce. They have been known to pull in the same harness together, even though the greatness that spurns the chariot of the arena mounts a solitary Pegasus. As Mr. Tarkington is a good writer as well as a good seller it leads to an understanding of him to think separately of why the many dote on him, and why some of the wise approve him.

II

In the early days of his authorship Mr. Tarkington made a start something like that of Clyde Fitch. Though they were both later to come back to their own neighborhoods, they were both enamored at the start—in *Beau Brummel* and *Monsieur Beaucaire*—with characters and backgrounds at a far remove from the worlds they lived in. When Tarkington was beginning there was a literary swing in this direction, so that it was altogether natural for him to fall in with Churchill and Ford and Major. And it was no less natural for him to fall in with James and Howells and

Mrs. Wharton by contributing his quota to the transatlantic novel in such stories as *The Guest of Quesnay* and *His Own People*. Yet in the latter he showed as early as 1907 an inclination to react to foreign impressions and experiences less in the manner of Howells than in the manner of Mark Twain. The author of *Innocents Abroad* wrote with the purpose "to suggest to the reader how *he* would be likely to see Europe and the East, if he looked at them with his own eyes instead of the eyes of those who traveled in those countries before him." The author of *His Own People* sent a Hoosier boy to the Continent, allowed him to make a fool of himself to the top of his bent, and brought him, through disillusionment by pseudo-genteel sharpers, to a realizing sense of the beauties and the innocents at home. Mr. Tarkington felt nothing but contempt for the squint of the anglo-maniac, but he felt a measure of sympathy for the short-sightedness of the Ohio Valley provincial who gloried in a county courthouse that could beat the worst ruined ruin in Italy.

The qualities of Indiana—both the charms of innocence and the aspects of guile—had already occupied him and were to occupy him more and more. On the side of innocence the stories of Penrod and William Sylvanus Baxter were the chief stepping-stones to his popularity. I dissent from the rather fatuous dictum that all the world loves a lover, for most of us are bored and embarrassed by him. But if it were actually true, and there were few things that the world loved more, two of them would be childhood and youth—at a comfortable distance. Mr. Tarkington gives his readers all the joys of a bachelor uncle, not the least of which is enjoying the discomfiture of parents from the pleasant vantage-point of celibacy. The parents of Mr. Tarkington's god-children have permanent responsibilities, and have inevitable contact with their offspring when they are dull or ill or cranky, as well as when they are whimsically interesting. But the readers of the Tarkington stories can enjoy the children at their best and disown them at will. It is the difference between darning stockings or hunting mittens and going to a perennial children's party in someone else's house. Naturally the world that could almost recite *Tom Sawyer* and *Huckleberry Finn* backward turned with zest to these fresh pages; and they enjoyed the stories page by page; how they came out is a matter of only the slightest interest.

On the other hand, how the tales of grown-up Indiana come out is a matter of very real moment; for it is a trait of the Tarkington novels, from the first almost to the last, that they end well. Russ Mellin, fooled and fleeced by continental sharpers, is reimbursed by one of the women, and sent home with a full purse. Joe Louden in *The Conquest of Canaan* is enabled to play the rôle of local reformer, and win a lovely bride to boot. Bibbs Sheridan of *The Turmoil*, utterly unqualified for business by both temperament and training, enters it on the failure of one older brother and the death of the other, and becomes a Titan over night. After being taught to love him for his amiably pathetic futility in a smoke-begrimed world, we are bidden to admire him as chief stoker. George Minafer, last and most insufferable of the magnificent Ambersons, although bereft of every vestige of claim to the reader's affection or respect, is awarded the heroine at the final curtain. The implication is that George is a sadder and a wiser man, and that he and his lady love will live happily ever after. The demonstrated fact is that he is an incorrigible snob, and that he can never rise to the level of the woman who is so nonchalantly tossed into his arms.

To anyone who is interested in stories not as narrative formulas—hero, heroine, obstacle, happy dénouement—but as the chronicles of natural people, the popular endings of the Tarkington novels are usually anything but pleasant. For Mr. Tarkington is a composite of sensitive tenderness and brutal disregard. He naturally inclines toward the finer sorts of people for whom the man on the street has little use. He develops them with sympathy and a great deal of insight, and he does it well enough to endear them to the reader who can understand them. The impractical idealist of **his** pages is a grown-up Willy Baxter; Tarkington makes a real man of him—like Bibbs Sheridan, for example. He develops more than one young woman of beauty and strength. He gives them a genuinely maternal wisdom and patience. But having brought them into being in the midst of the turmoil, he faces an awkward dilemma. He must let the story dispose of them as it will, or he must dispose of them himself as the man on the street and his sentimental daughter would prefer. This is according to the commercial formula, "to be prosperous is to be happy," or the romance formula, "to be married is to be happy." But, as a matter of fact, such a disposition is often an affront to the reader and a cruel injustice to the character. Bibbs loses his soul when he goes into business. George Minafer's bride is a living sacrifice. Yet it is quite apparent that Mr. Tarkington directed their fortunes out of a mistaken tenderness of heart, hoping for the best, and that the man on the street and his matinée daughter will be quite satisfied. As long as everything is pleasant when the curtain goes down. . . . .

Another reason for the popular acclaim of Mr. Tarkington is his ability to deal as amiably with period background as with character. And the two are very closely related. Penrod and Clarence rejoice their irresponsible uncles, not only because their endearing young charms are amusing in themselves, but because they are so amusingly like the boyhoods that their uncles look smilingly back to. Those boyhoods were spent somewhere from 1875 on, in social circumstances which have lapsed into a colorless half-oblivion except as someone with a vivid memory recalls them. Then the kindly smile of reminiscence rises. The illustrated section of the Sunday magazine capitalizes this feeling with its pictorial Do-You-Remember-Way-Back-When section. Mr. Tarkington makes a second appeal to his own generation in recalling the backgrounds as well as the years of their youth.

III

However, Mr. Tarkington has other qualities than those inherent in the salesmanship

that makes "best sellers." If he did not mark
the obvious distinction between mere popularity and solid excellence, Harold Bell
Wright, Edgar Guest, George M. Cohan, and
Dr. Frank Crane would be walking off with
the Pulitzer prizes.

He has a clear eye for character, and he
has created some that have won the widest
of reputations. Since the Dickens triumphs
of two generations ago Tom Sawyer has been
the only boy to gain a celebrity as general as
that of Mr. Tarkington's two protégés of
eleven and seventeen. As a matter of fact, in
these last two generations fiction in English
has failed to create more than two or three
characters to rival a dozen or a score of
Dickens'. Uncle Tom and Sherlock Holmes
are really well known. They could stand in
any newspaper headline. They mean as
much as any popular figure now living. But
there are no others. Wells with all his vogue
has not created one man or woman who is
known in ordinary talk; nor Galsworthy nor
Bennett nor Churchill, nor whoever you will
on this side the water—except Tarkington;

but you are safe in alluding to Penrod or to the boy who was Seventeen in any company.

It is in a measure true that these boys, and particularly the older one, have been presented for the benefit of older readers; but this comment has too often been made by critics as though it were an accusation instead of an appraisement; and, oddly enough, the same critics who have deplored Tarkington's softness of heart and sentimentalism in the matter of his plot-building, have deprecated his ironical and altogether unsentimental attitude toward childhood. They have apparently wanted to "get him going and coming," as if unwilling to be caught in the admission that he had done anything commendable of any kind. In forcing home this latter charge they have disparaged *Penrod* by citing *Tom Sawyer*. Yet Mark Twain frankly claimed for Tom the interest of his elders:

Although my book is intended mainly for the entertainment of boys and girls, I hope it will not be shunned by men and women on that account, for part of my plan has been to try to pleasantly remind adults of what they once were themselves, and of how they felt and thought and talked, and what queer enterprises they sometimes engaged in.

It is for this same reason in both Mark Twain and Booth Tarkington that teachers and parents have learned something about the childhood that is too near for them to see clearly. Dim memories of hearing "grand, gloomy and peculiar" spoken by a wise parent of two elder brothers who were about Billy Baxter's age when I was Penrod's never meant much to me until I read the much maligned stories about children for grown-ups. The points in these books are all doubt-less made in G. Stanley Hall's *Adolescence* (2 vols., octavo!), but there are still some parents who have not committed these vol-umes to memory.

In his descriptions of the middle-western town, Mr. Tarkington has been faithful as well as amusing. In the modern "revolt from the village"—Mr. Van Doren's inspired phrase—Mr. Masters and all his younger suc-cessors have presented true and truly depres-sing pictures of life. But there is no one picture and no one kind of picture that can give the whole truth about anything as complex as a whole community. Mr. Masters and Mr. Anderson see a great deal that is dark and devious and desperate in the average town; Mr. Lewis, much that is dull; and many alertly intellectual folk contend that dulness and stupidity mark the road to hell. Each of them has been as partial in his selection of material as Mr. Tarkington has.

If the novelist is subject to indictment unless he writes to champion a social thesis, then unintelligence should be presented as a tragic fact. But if the novelist has a right and a duty to present life as he sees it, then he is bound—if he sees them—to hold the mirror up to some of the vast majority of unthinking people who perhaps ought to be bored to the verge of suicide by the utter tameness of their lots, but who in truth are having a very good time with life because unfortunately they do not know enough to be unhappy. Mr. Tarkington has a special gift for the delineation of this stratum because the individuals in it are children in all but years, and because he has a native aptitude for drawing children; and he is able, as Mr. Howells was before him, to demonstrate that, after all, the degree of interest in human subject-matter is determined chiefly by the magnifying power of the lens through which it is seen. At the same time the author is indubitably bigger than his characters. His sympathy with them is usually tinged with irony. He understands their mental and emotional processes but never identifies himself with them. He is affectionate but detached.

So, too, he is with the region and the period of his boyhood that he thoroughly enjoys. Always there is in his feeling the combination of affection and conscious appraisal that we recall in Daniel Webster's attitude toward Dartmouth College or in Touchstone's toward Audrey. So in his treatment of the nineties, Mr. Tarkington sees them not merely in themselves but with the historian's realization of what they were moving away from and what they were drifting toward. In this spirit he presents the social side of the end of the century with the fashions in dress, the domestic architecture and ménage, the favorite dances, songs, and plays, the prevailing leisure:

In those days before deathly contrivances hustled them through their lives, and when they had no telephones . . . . they had time for everything; time to think, to talk, time to read, time to wait for a lady!

And the prevailing thrift:

Indeed their thrift was next to their religion, to save, even for the sake of saving, was their earliest lesson and discipline. No matter how prosperous they were, they could not spend money either upon "art" or upon mere luxury and entertainment without a sense of sin.

IV

Mr. Tarkington is neither an original nor an independent thinker. He is a not too searching realist, tinged with sentimentalism, and his mind is not unlike that of William Sylvanus Baxter's uncle. It is observant but untroubled by intense convictions. As an intelligent Hoosier of the twentieth century, this Mr. Baxter is in the main quiescent. America—the United States—is a residential district for him. He hardly thinks of it in terms either of allegiance or of obligation. It does not hold his attention any more than does the church, a multiplex institution with a series of meeting-houses among which the town is socially distributed. The family is the family, unchallengeable as the Ohio River, a placid stream rippling to eternity without falls or rapids, unruffled even by transverse winds. As an observer he seems to feel that life is well enough if only people will let it alone; but as they do not, he is made a little uneasy by such activities as those of the sordid and unwashed politician, or those of the ruthless captain of finance. On the whole, dear old Indiana is good enough for Mr. Baxter, and what is good enough for him ought to be good enough for the next generation. From which sentiments Mr. Tarkington shows no inclination to demur. Crowns and thrones may perish, Kingdoms rise and wane, But old Indiana, Constant shall remain.

He has been said never to have outgrown Princeton and Purdue. He has been a long time coming to it; but in his latest work

Mr. Tarkington has finally come to the point where he could leave his friends in the hands of fate, where he could doom them to the consequences of their own personalities. In *Alice Adams* there are no eleventh-hour reprieves. Perhaps he has turned a corner. If this proves to be the case the many will applaud him less, but the wise will approve him more.

BIOGRAPHICAL NOTE

Booth Tarkington was born in Indianapolis in 1869, the birth-year of Edwin Arlington Robinson and Edgar Lee Masters. The first strong literary influence exerted on him was that of his neighbor, James Whitcomb Riley, a writer who showed the rich interests inherent in Indiana conditions and Indiana people. He went to an eastern preparatory school, Phillips Exeter Academy, and to college at Purdue University, in his own state, and finally at Princeton University. At the latter he left a reputation as a developing writer, but is even better remembered as a singer, actor, and charming good fellow. After an unsuccessful start in art study, he gave himself up to writing. Success came with only moderate promptitude. It was six years from college graduation when his first book appeared in 1900, and seven before he achieved a notable success with *Monsieur Beaucaire*. Since then his progress has been steady; and his best work and his highest honors have come within the last two years.

Mr. Tarkington's publications are as follows: *The Gentleman from Indiana*, 1899; *Monsieur Beaucaire*, 1900; *The Two Vanrevels*, 1902; *Cherry*, 1903; *In the Arena*, 1905; *The Conquest of Canaan*, 1905; *The Beautiful Lady*, 1905; *His Own People*, 1907; *The Guest of Quesnay*, 1908; *Beasley's Christmas Party*, 1909; *Beauty and the Jacobin*, 1911; *The Flirt*, 1913; *Penrod*, 1914; *The Turmoil*, 1915; *Penrod and Sam*, 1916; *Seventeen*, 1916; *The Magnificent Ambersons*, 1918; *Ramsey Milholland*, 1919; *Clarence* (a play), 1919; *Alice Adams*, 1921; *The Intimate Strangers*, 1921; *Gentle Julia*, 1922; *The Midlander*, 1924.

The most important critical writings on Mr. Tarkington are by Robert C. Holliday, *Booth Tarkington* (a volume); W. P. Eaton in *At the New Theatre;* Meredith Nicholson in *The Hoosiers;* Carl Van Doren in *Contemporary American Novelists;* and Edith Wyatt in the *North American Review* for October, 1922.

VIII

Theodore Dreiser

I

THEODORE DREISER, like his an-
tithesis, Mr. Cabell, is under great
debt to his foes, for both have come
into general repute by the avenue of notoriety. The time still seems millenniums away
when the zealous guardians of tradition will
understand that repressive tactics are always
self-defeated, always immeasurably the best
advertisers and stimulants that anything with
the smallest title to social existence could
desire. But it is in the nature of repressors
to be so short-sighted that the thought of a
nude picture banished to the ash-pile or the
storeroom, a piece of printing barred from
the library or the mails, or a conscientious
objector in solitary confinement, looms larger
than the thought of the inevitable reaction
such a challenge to the public will bring

about. They have never understood the stories of Pandora and of Bluebeard's wife. Nothing can convince the censors that the public is just as certain to pry and peek into forbidden places as these two very amiably human ladies were. So they continue to educate the public in questions of art and letters, and freedom of expression in general, and probably, in the end, do far more for the cause of free speech than they could contrive to do in any other way.

In 1900 Dreiser's *Sister Carrie* was issued by a New York publisher and on second thought suppressed by him. It was the same year in which Zola's *Fecundity* was published and widely circulated. Dreiser says:

> We were not used then in America to calling a spade a spade, particularly in books. We had great admiration for Tolstoi and Flaubert and Balzac and De Maupassant at a distance . . . . but mostly we had been schooled to the literature of . . . . that refined company of English sentimental realists who told us something about life, but not everything.

Eleven years later *Jennie Gerhardt* appeared and caused a great deal of comment, resuscitating *Sister Carrie*, so that Dreiser now had the advantage of a double-barreled attack. People were amazed. Whether they were delighted or perturbed depended on their moral and artistic predispositions; but they were all agog. In the meanwhile, eleven years had done much to sophisticate the American reader, but, fortunately for Dreiser's sales, not quite enough to make him acceptable as a matter of course. So new objections were raised, as they were later to *The Genius*, Dreiser was barred, hither and yon, from school and village libraries—and his reputation was established. The Caliban of contemporary fiction!

As this tempest was taking its course, the career of Ferdinand was also quietly developing. Mr. Cabell had been writing voluminously for the periodicals, but without wide recognition. Novels, tales, and poems were coming along in book form from a comparatively unknown publishing-house. Even *The Rivet in Grandfather's Neck* and *The Cream of the Jest*, of 1913 and 1917—books which their author has not yet surpassed—were quite overlooked by the buyers of best sellers and the dinner-table critics. But when *Jurgen* appeared and was suppressed in 1919, not by its own publisher, but by a society for the suppression of vice, and when with lifted eyebrow and lowered voice it was branded as phallic literature, collectors paid as high as forty dollars for copies, critics in article after article began discussing not *Jurgen* alone but the whole course and value of Cabell's work, Hugh Walpole paid him the tribute of a bookful of appraisal; and when the legal ban was removed, *Jurgen* was displayed in the window of every enterprising bookseller, and the author put in a position to enlarge the herd at Dumbarton Grange. Ferdinand had appeared on the scene, and ten thousand Mirandas were enthralled.

So much for repression.

II

The jury of the critics is divided. The most aggressively conservative says Dreiser has told us just two things about his favorite male character: that he has a rapacious appetite for wealth and for women, and that the books about this man are in effect huge club sandwiches "composed of slices of business alternating with erotic episodes." The most rampant champion retorts on the "critical imbecility which detects naught save a tom-cat in Frank Cowperwood." And a third critic, who is more concerned to understand Dreiser than to dispose of opposite views, says that the novelist is a mystic who employs the gestures of the realist. Clearly Dreiser has come to stay, and must be reckoned with.

In the circumstances, there is no better way to begin the reckoning than to ask what he writes about.

To anyone who has had Dreiser held up to him as a kind of moral ghoul, obsessed with animalism, the reading of *Twelve Men* will come with a series of surprises as upsetting as the shocks would be if he read one of the novels with his tastes all prepared for the output of Louisa May Alcott. By implica-tion this book of biographical portraits is highly—and I should think to the ultra-moderns, offensively—moralistic. Peter is a gay lover of life who reaches his self-fulfil-ment as the incarnation of faithful domesti-city; Charlie Potter is "just a good man, that's all"; Paul Dresser is jovial, good-hearted unselfishness in the flesh, three hun-dred pounds of it; Dr. Gridley is the servant of the whole countryside. Almost every one of the twelve, to use Dreiser's own formula

. . . . deliberately and of choice holds fast to many, many simple and human things, and rounds out life, or would, in a natural, normal, courageous, healthy way.

As portraits these men are taken out of their surroundings, or at least distinguished from them; but in the five novels which rep-resent the author's most ambitious attempt to present life, men and women are put in the midst of a multitudinous world, and become manikins played with by forces which they can never control and to which they are usually unable to adjust themselves. It is a grim world, but the grimness comes less from the sight and the thought of social hardship than from the consciousness of ruthless, supernatural forces. The central characters in the novels are externally successful. Sister Carrie, from Columbia City, Wisconsin, is started on what the reader may expect to be the road to ruin; but borne on the tide of circumstance, she is lifted out of penurious labor, and out of the pitfalls of love without benefit of clergy, to success on the stage and to a condition of life in which there are no devastating traces of the upward struggle. Nor is she a stricken soul at the end. Sitting in her luxurious quarters, still young and still lovely, she sings and dreams, knowing neither surfeit nor content; but dreaming and doomed to strive always for a happiness she may never reach. Frank Cowperwood, hero of the trilogy of desire, is born to conquest—master and squanderer of many fortunes and many loves. The poetic justice of literary tradition would do with him what it did with Hurstwood, buccaneer in *Sister Carrie*, crushing him at the end; but the last glimpse of him reveals him not punished, but rewarded with his latest love, and departing for fresh victories in new financial fields. The genius Witla achieves brilliantly, though all the while he is a puppet in the hands of fate, impelled to create beauty, just as Cowperwood is to amass fortunes, and Sister Carrie to allure admirers. They all seem to have power; yet in fact they are all powerless to control the energies with which they are endowed.

To make this the clearer, Dreiser immerses them in the tumultuous life of the big city: at the top, the privileged few of the inner social circle; below these, the bohemian world of artist, actor, author, and dilettante; then the makers of money, builders of fine houses, buyers of libraries and pictures, manipulators of law, and ignorers (in fact, if not in pretense) of gospel; finally, the substratum of the millions in factory, railroad, and shipyard, upholding all the rest, but fundamentally no less happy than those whom they uphold, since none can ever experience for long either surfeit or contentment.

III

In "De Maupassant, Jr.," one of the *Twelve Men*, Dreiser writes interestingly of a young author (was it Stephen Crane?) who at first had no conception of structure in writing, but who "seemed finally to grasp the theory I had, or at least to develop a method of his own which was quite as satisfactory to me." Just what this theory of structure may have been is not so easy for one of Dreiser's readers to grasp as it was for the young aspirant; for in the main his stories are as shapeless as Polyphemus, huge, ungainly, bristling, blind in one eye. In certain of the shorter units there is a definite turn of outline and something like a contour. For the formlessness of the novels the cue is perhaps supplied in a further comment on the youthful De Maupassant, who was "no namby-pamby scribbler of the old happy-ending, pretty-nothing school of literary composition."

Dreiser is not only not a happy-ending novelist; he is equally not a tragic-ending story-teller. He writes to a theme rather than to a plot. When you have withdrawn a little way from one of his stout books, memory makes clear an inevitable direction in it and throughout it; but while you are in the midst of it you need a clear head to maintain a sense of anything more than a whirling turbulent, on-crowding tide, covered with flotsam and jetsam. In *The Financier* and *The Titan*, for example, there is no fusing of either of the cities into a definite set of characters through whom the main elements are represented. One experience after another brings you into fresh contact with hitherto unmentioned men and women. The stories do not move on as life does, for in actual life the people with whom a man will some day be involved come gradually into his consciousness before they share his destiny. Halfway through *The Titan*, and long after Cowperwood has begun playing with political pawns, he comes to a point where he needs to deal with more powerful men. Chapter xxxv begins:

In the first and second wards of Chicago at this time were two men . . . . who for picturesqueness of character and sordidness of atmosphere could not be equaled elsewhere in the city, if in the nation at large.

Several thousand words of characterization follow. It is typical Dreiserian structure, except that in this instance the characterization is dramatic and interesting, whereas it is often heavy, conscientious, unrelieved.

And this untrammeled desire to explain is naturally harnessed with an almost total inability to suggest. An epilogue expounds the trend of a story. Interjected comments expound character after character and action after action. Parentheses interpolate cautions against missing points that are quite obvious. Acquainted with Cowperwood through one whole volume and 122 pages of another, we are yet informed that "his nature concealed (under a very forceful exterior) a deep, underlying element of romance and fire." His wife, in a jealous rage, calls one rival "a thin stick," another "a little piece of gum," a third "a dead fish"; and we are informed: "(Aileen had a genius for characterization at times)."

Perhaps it is just as well that Dreiser does not attempt to work through suggestion, because it is the essence of this sort of indirect discourse that it be deft, with happy phrasing, skilful allusion, and firmly handled metaphor and simile. But Dreiser is a Flemish artist. He is quite capable of spending two weeks on a broom-handle. Furthermore, while he is piling up his vast accumulation of unselected detail, he writes clumsily, badly at times. What shall one say of such as these: "He wondered when, if ever, this story was to culminate, let alone he write it"? "I cannot understand why people cling so fatuitously to the idea"? Or of so extraordinarily mixed a metaphor as that which describes the Woolworth Building as lifting "its defiant spear of clay into the very maw of heaven"? No Hamlet could ever have said to Dreiser: "More matter and less art." And yet, scattered here and there all along his pages are passages of a fine and simple and rhythmic beauty. *Hey Rub-a-Dub-Dub* is full of them:

What has impressed me most about life, always, is the freshness and newness of everything, the perennial upwelling of life in every form; the manner in which, as age steals on for some, youth, new, innocent, inexperienced, believing, takes charge, its eyes alight with aspiration, its body ablaze with desire, ... Does the bit of thread or pattern that we see here now, show the least evidence of wear or tear? Is not the race as new, as fresh as ever? We rise betimes, and the ancient sunlight streams fresh and strong and *new* into our passing window—this window, which, in a few years, will be as forgotten and as unrecoverable as we ourselves shall be.

IV

This is Emersonian, in tone as well as quality; for, oddly enough, in view of Dreiser's chief panegyrists, Dreiser's philosophy is a balance between Emerson's and Mark Twain's, and in its vein of hope, much nearer to the Concord optimist's than to the pessimist's of Stormfield. Like both these men, and like Walt Whitman, too, Dreiser has no philosophical formula, but is a continual asker of questions. "I am one of those curious persons who cannot make up their minds about anything." As a youth he had been like the reporter he tells of in *Nigger Jeff*, who up to the time of a lynching assignment had been "a rather self-sufficient youth who was inclined to be of the turn of mind which

sees in life only a fixed and ordered process
of rewards and punishments," but who came
at the end of his day's work to the conviction that "it was not always exact justice
that was meted out to all, and that it was
not so much the business of the writer to
indict as to interpret." In another place
Dreiser has told of this same shift in point
of view in terms still more direct:

About this time I read the *Data of Ethics* and *First
Principles* of Herbert Spencer. They nearly killed me,
took every shred of belief away from me; showed me
that I was a chemical atom in a whirl of unknown
forces; the realization clouded my mind. I felt the
rhythm of life, but the central fact to me was that the
whole thing was unknowable—incomprehensible. I
went into the depths and I am not sure that I have ever
got entirely out of them

In the sense of feeling no certainty as to the
underlying laws of life, he is an agnostic, like
Mark Twain; but in his incessant effort to
reach solid ground, and his desire to tread
confidently on it, he is at one with Emerson
and Whitman. He is perplexed by "this mad
chaos of fraud, frivolity, and hoggishness"
which we call life, but he is not dismayed by

it. He seems to think that he subscribes
to the mechanistic theory—popularly "Dar-
winism"—"survival of the species, adaptation, and all their other evolution terms,"
a theory which puts the individual helpless
in the midst of a vast process remorselessly
grinding toward some undetermined future.
Yet over and over again he hints at the sus-
picion that will not down in him, that there
is an inward, impelling force pushing mankind upward as well as onward.

Again and again he explicitly rejects the
existence of justice and morality, yet he
never stops groping to find what he calls
"the equation inevitable." The earth, he
says, is populated with giants and pygmies;
the giants eat the pygmies if they can. They
leave devastation in their train, and, in
strange irony, monuments to beauty, too.
But he falls back on law after all in an Emersonian resort to compensation.

In the end a balance is invariably struck wherein
the mass subdues the individual or the individual the
mass—for the time being. For, behold, the sea is ever

dancing or raging. In the meantime there have sprung up social words and phrases expressing a need of balance—of equation. These are right, justice, truth, morality, an honest mind, a pure heart—all words meaning a balance must be struck.

These social words, repudiate them how he may, are the nearest substitute for the Rock of Ages that he can find, and he is continually clambering back to them as the sea dances and rages.

The parallel may be carried farther without undue forcing. Dreiser is comparable to Emerson again in his insistence on the right of the individual to live his own life, and to cast behind him all conformity. Here is a passage from each. Assign them if you can:

> If you maintain a dead church, contribute to a dead Bible society, vote with a great party, either for the government or against it, spread your table like base housekeepers—under all these screens I have difficulty to detect the precise man you are.

> Not to cling too pathetically to a religion or a system of government or a theory of morals or a method of living, but to be ready to abandon at a moment's notice, is the apparent teaching of the ages.

To go a step farther still, their views even on the theory of obligations of person to person are not in conflict. Says Emerson:

> If you are noble, I will love you; if you are not, I will not hurt you and myself by hypocritical attentions. If you are true, but not in the same truth with me, cleave to your companions; I will seek my own. I do this not selfishly but humbly and truly. It is alike your interest and mine, and all men's, however long we have dwelt in lies, to live in truth.

Dreiser could hardly say more.

This is not to contend that Dreiser and Emerson are alike. The point is that the difference between them is not in their fundamental views but in their applications of them. In living Emerson was the most conventional of men; Dreiser has never pretended to conform. In literature Emerson confined himself to the abstract. Dreiser in his novels not only expresses himself in the concrete but with the concreteness of naturalism. In his essay on "Love," Emerson developed just the distinction between himself and his uncouth successor, while giving a character to the latter's work:

Theodore Dreiser

Everything is beautiful seen from the point of the intellect, or as truth. But all is sour if seen from experience. Details are melancholy; the plan is seemly and noble. In the actual world—the painful kingdom of time and place—dwell care and canker and fear.

In this painful kingdom Dreiser is doing a work as massive and hard-wrought as the statues of Rodin. If it is the business of the critic to interpret rather than to indict, we must admit that the failure of his characters to round out their lives in "a natural, normal, courageous, healthy way" is because he feels it his artistic duty to write of the actual world. Yet behind it all there is a wistful yearning for something better that only perverse blindness can fail to perceive.

BIOGRAPHICAL NOTE

Theodore Dreiser was born in Terre Haute, Indiana, in 1871. His parents were German-Americans; an older brother, Paul, won prosperous celebrity as a composer of popular songs. Dreiser was educated in the public schools of Warsaw, Indiana, and in the state university. From 1892 to 1910 he was engaged in journalistic work, first on newspapers in Chicago and St. Louis; as editor of *Every Month*, a literary and musical magazine, 1895–98; as contributor to *Harper's*,

McClure's, Munsey's, the *Cosmopolitan*, and the *Century*, 1898–1906; and as editor-in-chief of the Butterick publications: the *Delineator, Designer, New Idea*, and *English Delineator*, 1907–10. He lives in New York City and devotes himself entirely to writing. Interesting autobiographic material is contained in *Hey Rub-a-Dub-Dub, Twelve Men, A Traveler at Forty, A Hoosier Holiday*, and *A Book about Myself*.

His publications have been as follows: *Sister Carrie*, 1900; *Jennie Gerhardt*, 1911; *The Financier*, 1912; *A Traveler at Forty* (travel sketches), 1913; *The Titan*, 1914; *The Genius*, 1915; *Plays of the Natural and Supernatural*, 1916; *A Hoosier Holiday*, 1916; *Free and Other Stories*, 1918; *The Hand of the Potter* (a play), 1918; *Twelve Men* (biographical studies), 1919; *Hey Rub-a-Dub-Dub*, 1920; *A Book about Myself*, 1922; *The Color of a Great City*, 1923.

The most important critical articles are: Frank Harris, in *Contemporary Portraits;* H. L. Mencken, in *A Book of Prefaces;* Stuart P. Sherman, in *On Contemporary Literature;* Carl Van Doren, in *Contemporary American Novelists.*

IX

Mr. Cabell Expounds Himself

I

M R. CABELL demands a place in any short series on American contemporary writers because he is the most aggressive and most talked-of romantic novelist in the country, just as Mr. Dreiser must needs have a hearing because he is the most relentless realist. Dreiser believes in telling the whole truth about life and he finds the truth on every hand, revealed to the physical eye; Cabell contends that the only truth that is tolerable is the truth that repudiates the sordid and homely and wearisome facts of daily life. Dreiser's style is as homely as his material; Cabell's as ornate as his romantic dream-world. Dreiser's whole life has been identified with certain great northern cities, Cabell's with southern towns—

Chicago versus Lichfield. Dreiser is a Puritan apostate—recalcitrant, but still a Puritan in tradition; Cabell is a Cavalier. There is only one point at which they agree—their dissent from the established conventional code, the rule of Mrs. Grundy; Dreiser ignores her or pushes her aside without apology, but Cabell is acutely aware that she is present, and takes a malicious pleasure in annoying her. Knowing that it would be useless to poison her soup, he at least seeks the satisfaction of spoiling her appetite.

Because of their common contempt for the old lady they have acquired much the same set of hostile critics; and the fierce assault on them both, one cannot help believing, has acquired for them the same set of champions. Mr. Cabell's assailants have gone to lengths which remind one of the good old days of short and ugly words. Probably no American author since Cooper has been more roundly abused: "Slushy and disgusting," "Worse than immoral—dull," "Revolting," "A boudoir budget," "Hardly excusable in print," "The whine of a little old man," and the culminating censoring of *Jurgen*. It is a kind of vituperation that has made defenders of Cabell even where it has not made genuine friends for him.

II

The discussion of Cabell's literary ways and works is not limited to what friends and foes have said about him, for he is a prolific commentator on himself. In the person of certain story-spokesmen, notably Manuel and Jurgen, Robert Townsend, Felix Kennaston, and John Charteris, he states his case in scores of passages and dozens of ways. He has little patience for the methods of the realist:

No one on the preferable side of Bedlam wishes to be reminded of what we are in actuality, even were it possible, by any disastrous miracle, ever to dispel the mist which romance has evoked about all human doings.

Says Charteris:

If ever I were to attempt a tale of Lichfield, I would not write a romance, but a tragedy. I think I would call my tragedy *Futility*, for it would mirror the life of Lichfield with unengaging candor; and, as a consequence, people would complain that my tragedy lacked sustained interest, and that its participants were inconsistent; that it had no ordered plot, no startling incidents, no high endeavors, and no special aim; and that it was equally deficient in all time-hallowed provocatives of either laughter or tears.

This fairly characterizes the two stories of Lichfield which Mr. Cabell wrote, *Cords of Vanity* and *The Rivet in Grandfather's Neck* (the remarks of Charteris come from the latter), though the author, instead of labeling them tragedies, sardonically calls one "A Comedy of Shirking" and the other "A Comedy of Limitations."

In *The Cream of the Jest*, Horvendile—one of Mr. Cabell's two disguises in this book—takes up the theme:

There was once in a land very far away from this land—in my country—a writer of romances. And once he constructed a romance, which, after a hackneyed custom of my country, purported to be translated from an old manuscript. . . . . I am that writer of romance. This room, this castle, all the broad, rolling country-side without, is but a portion of my dream, and these places have no existence save in my fancies. . . . . I find my country an inadequate place in which to live. . . . . There is that in some of us which gets no exercise there; and we struggle blindly, with impotent yearning, to gain outlet for great powers which we know that we possess, even though we do not know their names. And so, we dreamers wander at adventure to Storisende—oh, and into more perilous realms sometimes!—in search of a life that will find employment for every faculty that we have.

Storisende is in Cabell's Poictesme, "which is bounded by Avalon and Phaeacia and sea-coast Bohemia, and the contiguous forests of Arden and Broceliande, and on the west of course by the Hesperides," a country which he believes "to be the one possible setting for a really satisfactory novel, even though its byways can boast of little traffic nowadays." However, he does not confine his characters to even an imaginary realm. They wander in all directions—to Alexandria, Aquitaine, Arcadia, Asgard, to Barbary, England, Jerusalem, Massilia, to Navarre, Olympus, Portugal, and Rome. And they cover all chronology in their orbit around the thirteenth century from which most of their beautiful happenings are supposed to spring. "Homer dreamed of you," says one of his lovers to one of his loved ones, "and Sophocles and Theocritus. All poets

have had glimpses of you." So he relates
heroes and heroines in genealogies as inventive as his maps, and on a slender thread of heritage strings his garlands of slender stories,
reaching through the ages, all dealing with
the chivalric search for the unattainable, or
with the gallant acceptance of the pleasures
and inconveniences of life.

III

Mr. Cabell's avowed intention is "to
write perfectly about beautiful happenings."
To do this is not for him to achieve a perfect
technique and then to exercise it with natural and spontaneous zest. He is a laborious
pleasure-hunter. His style is like his use of
geography and genealogy, and his partly
actual and partly invented authorities. It
is like the painstaking play in words—the
jest of the cream in *The Cream of the Jest*—
which is wrought out concerning the sigil
of Scoteia. Throughout the book it is described as a bit of metal with the magic
power of invoking a dream-life. At the end
of the story it is explained as being only one-

half of the broken top of a cold-cream jar marked with a design made up by "blending meaningless curlicues and dots and circles with an irresponsible hand." Yet in a blank page before the title is a cut of the bit of metal; and the Cabell enthusiast who owns the copy before me has painfully deciphered the marks, which are upside down in the book, and which declare that "James Branch Cabell made this book, etc., etc." A deal of work for so slight a conclusion! One is by this time ready to believe that the inscription thus deciphered is in itself a code, and that the quintessence of the cream has yet to be extracted.

There is the same evidence of unstinted pains in the prose style; and one deplores, of course, not the pains, but the evidence thereof. It is all wrought out by hard plodding, no step of which is easier for all that have been taken before it. He writes of proofreading:

Here was the word vexatiously repeated within three lines, which must be replaced by a synonym; and the clause which, when transposed, made the whole sentence gain in force and comeliness . . . .

and the vaguely unsatisfactory adjective, for which a jet of inspiration suggested a substitute.

Not always inspiration, either, for:

> Then you dip into an *Unabridged*, and change every word that has been written for a better one, and do it leisurely, rolling in the mouth, as it were, the flavour of every possible synonym, before decision. Then you reread with a corrective pen in hand the while, and you venture upon the whole to agree with Mérimée that it is preferable to write one's own books, since those of others are not, after all, particularly worth reading in comparison.

Such processes do not lead to any spontaneity of effect, and you do not find it in Mr. Cabell's pages. But he has anticipated criticism in his comments on Felix Kennaston, his (as he might put it) so obviously autobiographic character.

> His high-pitched voice in talking, to begin with, was irritating; you knew it was not his natural voice, and found it so entirely senseless for him to speak thus. Then, too, the nervous and trivial grin with which he prefaced almost all his infrequent remarks . . . . was peculiarly uningratiating.

Translated into prose style, these characteristics are Mr. Cabell's own on the printed page; though he ingeniously overstates the indictment and so forces whoever quotes it to become an attorney for the defense by deprecating its severity even while indorsing its pertinence.

His own style is indubitably established, though it must be remembered that he writes sometimes as himself and very often in the manner of this, that, or the other author of whom he is evidently reminded. For himself he tends to long sentences, frequently periodic, with interjected parentheses, inserted modifiers, inverted and transposed members. He is consciously suggestive of archaism without being too archaic; and he depends for relief on the introduction of marked and homely modernisms. On the whole, the style is attractive; sometimes it is charming. But certain mannerisms, like those of Kennaston's speech, are monotonously irritating. One wearies of the thousand-fold repetition of "a little by a little," "by ordinary," and the preciosity of his pet adverbs "kindlily" and "friendlily." This is unnecessarilily pedantic. He is pedantic, too, in the parading of his real and his imaginary sources. His stories are overloaded with display of historical precision. Knowing that, on the whole, fancy is more important than fact to the author, the reader is annoyed and distracted by circumstantial matters of chronology and genealogy that delay action and throw no light on motive. He might well have taken a leaf out of a book of Howard Pyle, with whom he was early associated, and have emulated his elder's lucid mastery of the Robin Hood legend.

IV

Mr. Cabell is a complete Virginian, which fact alone is enough to account for his love of fine and stately tradition. Only South Carolina would dare challenge Virginia's right to be considered the sum and substance of the South; but Virginia alone has the effrontery to take itself as seriously as South Carolina does; and the rest of the world takes it a little more so. They are both reminiscent states. (As, for that matter, Massachusetts and Connecticut are today—a free concession to any sensitive southerners.) However, the reminiscent quality of the South is of two very distinct and highly contrastable kinds: its romantic chivalry turns back to a remote and idealized past; but its own gallant self reverts to a much nearer, quite disillusion-ized, and sophisticated eighteenth century— two sources that are worthy of more than a moment's consideration.

The remote past, and the idealized life to be found there, is the genuine Age of Chiv-alry—"a world-wide code in consonance with which all estimable people lived and died. Its root was the assumption (uncon-tested then) that a gentleman will always serve his God, his honor, and his lady with-out any reservation." It was a code under which gentlemen and ladies regarded them-selves as children of an indulgent Father who was certain to deal out justice tempered with mercy; a code which later centuries com-pletely outgrew, but which in former times served society for a long while. It is the code which prevails in *Domnei*, a really beau-tiful story of sublimated love; and to it, in certain hours of disaffection with the modern "tragi-comic melée," the romantically disposed modern mind reverts with almost religious devotion. Such a reversion is possible only to those who can make it at a single, bold stride. The seeker for romantic relief must strip himself of every vestige of newworldliness, and lend himself without reserve to the "willing suspension of disbelief" which is necessary to an adoption of the chivalric code. This done, such a book as *Domnei* becomes readable and credible, a fine fruit of southern romantic faith. To fall short of this will result in *A Connecticut Yankee at the Court of King Arthur*, a natural product of northern romantic skepticism.

If, however, one lack seven-century boots and if one be conscious of the road back to medievalism, he falls on evil times, even in Virginia; for on the way he must pass through the eighteenth century, which is the parent of southern gallantry. What such a parentage means with respect to the romantic inheritance is revealed if we recall that the satirical *Rape of the Lock* was one of the early expressions and the ironic *Sense and Sensibility* a posthumous message. Whatever the contributory origins of southern speech and manners may be, they still resemble in some measure those that we associate with the days of Pope and Sterne and Jane Austen. Both are marked by a somewhat elevated formality of phrasing, an inclination to speak as from the rostrum, an opulent show of deference to beauty and woman, a vocal insistence upon honor and chivalry, and the stagey insincerity which follows hard on the heels of conventionalized forms of speech. He who talks the language of gallantry today in America can do it in only two ways: with the kindly smile of one who dances a minuet as a charming social accomplishment that no one takes seriously, or with the covert contempt of one who is talking to gullible inferiors. It is gallantry with its tongue in its cheek, and it is perfectly expressed in *Cords of Vanity, a Comedy of Shirking.*

Mr. Cabell's approach to life is not so uncomplicated that it may be summed up in either woman worship, which is chivalry in perfection, as in *Domnei*, or shirking, which is chivalry degenerate, as in *Cords of Vanity*. The greater part of his writing lies in the no-man's-land between. Of the stories of Poic-tesme, his ancient world, most are written with an ill-concealed smile, if not, as in the case of *Jurgen*, with a smirk. They are ro-mances of two worlds, ostensibly about an ancient one, but seen with modern eyes. Thus the "epistle dedicatory" of *The Line of Love* is addressed to Mrs. Grundy. This is minuet dancing at a fancy-dress ball—all very pretty, but only pseudo-romance. Of the stories of modern Virginia no other is so total a repudiation of chivalry as *Cords of Vanity*. In *The Rivet in Grandfather's Neck*, Rudolph Musgrave is a gentleman under the skin; but the code in this and the others seems to be that a gentleman may ignore his God, and may serve his honor and his lady only whenever it is agreeable and convenient.

One book marks the balancing of the two worlds—*The Cream of the Jest*—in which Felix Kennaston, author, lives corporeally in a twentieth-century world, acquires two motor cars, money in four banks, an enlarged waist-band, and a yearning for the romance which he finds nowhere about him. By means of his magic charm he is enabled to make off nightly to a world of dreams and idyllic adventure. Everywhere, even in this world, he sees men and women scurrying through a jungle of confused circumstance, "like feeble-minded ants," where he, and he only, can see the awe-inspiring design. Thrilled with the sense of beauty and order to which he is blinded in Lichfield, he is buoyed through days of unimportant tasks and tedious, use-less little habits. So, returning to daily life with the mocking sophistication of an eighteenth-century-derived Virginian, he yet carries back with him enough of the chival-ric code to be true to his love—disavowing loyalty even while he practices it; and to his Christian God—as a proof of confidence in his literary abilities; and between the two, quite incidentally of course, to his own honor.

At the outset I quoted some of the epithets applied to Mr. Cabell by his best enemies. His most effusive friends, writing introductions to his works by request, are equally immoderate: "*Beyond Life* is on the threshold of its day as the *Sartor Resartus* of modernism." "In *Figures of Earth* he undertook the staggering and almost unsuspected task of rewriting humanity's sacred books." "The magnificent writing that is visible on every page." I cannot see the need of considering him as either arch-fiend or demi-god. The most admirable thing about him has been his persistence in writing his own kind of novel in his own way until through ability and accident he has achieved a wide hearing. He ought to be taken as seriously as he takes life—with a touch of tolerant skepticism. His prevailing mood is the youthful vanity of Robert Townsend:

"That," I airily said, "is, in the first place, something you had no business to read; and, in the second, simply the blocking out of an entrancingly beautiful poem. It represents a mood."

"It is the sort of mood that isn't good for people, especially for children. It very often gets them shot full of large and very untidy holes."

"Nonsense!" said I, but not in displeasure, because it made me feel like such a devil of a fellow.

Mr. Cabell Expounds Himself

BIOGRAPHICAL NOTE

James Branch Cabell was born in Richmond, Virginia, in 1879. His parents belonged to old Virginia families and his own interest in genealogy is marked. He graduated from College of William and Mary in 1898, and was in newspaper work for the next three years. From 1902 to 1910 he wrote for the magazines, contributing some sixty short stories in addition to verse, translations, essays, and papers on historical and biographical subjects. From 1904 to 1919 he also published volumes at the rate of one every two years. With the notoriety which came with the stupid censoring of *Jurgen*, his output was doubled and his audience multiplied manifold. He lives on a country place in his native state.

His publications have been as follows: *The Eagle's Shadow*, 1904; *The Line of Love*, 1905; *Gallantry*, 1907; *Chivalry*, 1909; *The Cords of Vanity*, 1909; *The Soul of Melicent*, 1913; *The Rivet in Grandfather's Neck*, 1915; *The Certain Hour*, 1916; *From the Hidden Way* (verse), 1916; *The Cream of the Jest*, 1917; *Jurgen*, 1919; *Beyond Life* (essays), 1919; *The Cords of Vanity* (revised), 1920; *Domnei* (new version of *The Soul of Melicent*), 1920; *The Judging of Jurgen*, 1920; *Figures of Earth*, 1921; *Taboo*, 1921; *High Place*, 1923.

The most important critical articles are: Hugh Walpole, *The Art of James Branch Cabell* (a volume); Carl Van Doren, in *Contemporary American Novelists;* Robert Morss Lovett, in the *New Republic*, April 13, 1921.

X

Willa Cather

IF ONE were to speculate on what might be the literary output of a woman born in Virginia, diploma'd from a western state university in the nineties, schooled in an eastern newspaper office, and graduated from the staff of a popular monthly with metropolitan headquarters and a national circulation, it would be safe to look for some copiousness of material and some breadth of sympathy. And these are the characteristics of Miss Cather's work. Probably they are accounted for by her experience; at any rate they are true of her. The temptation is strong to pursue the theory that Miss Cather is the product of her changing backgrounds because her "Life and Works" are so typically related. More often than not maturing artistry comes into its own by slow degrees, starting with conventional form and conventional subject-matter, and only tardily arriving at individual style and substance. That is what accounts for Fielding's imposing array of early comedies, Scott's excursions into poetic romance, Poe's Byronic *Tamerlane* and *Politian;* and Hawthorne's contributions to the sentimental annuals. Maturity and achievement lead genuine creative ability (as it led all these men) back toward fundamentals and into the literary form in which it can best express itself.

Miss Cather's first book was a typical "slender volume" of poems published in 1903 when poetry in America was a pleasant parlor accomplishment. The reprint of twenty years later, even with its additions, is still slender in both size and content. There are verses of homely sentiment, classical echoes, Shakesperian, Arthurian, Italian, Provençal verses of allusion, reminiscences of travel, laments for lost loves and lost youth, and, among them all, three or four bits that are unbookish with the breath of prairies in them. Next, two years later, appeared *The Troll Garden*, seven stories—

artists' colony stories, painters, musicians, and music lovers in New York, Boston, and London, and among them three with allusions to western life, with one grim picture of a little Kansas town to which a sculptor is brought for burial, contemned in life as in death by the sordid villagers. Then, in Miss Cather's roster, after a seven-year interval which seems to have been largely absorbed by editorial routine, came two volumes, international or transatlantic, apparently pointing her way down the paths often traversed by Henry James and Mrs. Wharton. All the books so far were the work of a lover of beauty who had grown up among spiritually arid rural surroundings, who was thrilled by all the possibilities for beauty in studio and concert hall, and somewhat allured by the engaging artificialities of polite metropolitan life. The only life that occupied Miss Cather thus far was a life of aesthetic self-realization.

With a difference, as much may be said of her work as a whole, the difference being that in the mature novels the focus of her work shifted from the happy enjoyment of self-realization to the harrowing struggle toward that end. *O Pioneers* (1913) and *The Song of the Lark* (1915) marked Miss Cather's indubitable "arrival," although it was not until *My Ántonia* (1918) that this important event was generally recognized. With these books, as with the greater part of *One of Ours* (1922), she turned back to the richest of her sources, the pioneer figures of the prairie town, and in her employment of this material applied the principle which she ascribed to the lark who caroled so divinely, that "art is only a way of remembering youth." And thus one comes to that trio of heroic women—Alexandra Bergson, Thea Kronburg, and Ántonia Shimerda.

Of the stories centering around these three, *The Song of the Lark*, the chronicle of Thea Kronburg, is perhaps the least effective for the very reason that it is most explicitly given over to the struggle for artistic self-fulfilment. Thea Kronburg, daughter of a smugly complacent country parson and of a prolific and instinctively wise mother, grows up a solitary in the midst of a crowded household in a gossipy town. By natural gravitation she finds her happiest companionship with a broken-down, half-ostracized German music master, and with a song-loving colony of Mexican outcasts. To please her father, whom she has no wish to offend or estrange, she plays the hymns at the midweek prayer meetings, though she finds no relief there from the muffling and numbing daily clamor about her, and always reads late after the recital of prayers and "experiences," yearning more avidly than usual to live with zest and to achieve some real happiness.

Under the old music master's monitions she toils doggedly. An instinct in her responds natively to his precept that "nothing is far and nothing is near if one desires. The world is little, people are little, human life is little. There is only one big thing—desire. And before it, when it is big, all is little." She needs only look within herself to know all of what he means when he declares: "The secret—what make the rose

to red, the sky to blue, the man to love
—in der Brust, in der Brust it is, und ohne
dieses giebt es keine Kunst, keine Kunst!"
Toward this Parnassian art, then, she aspires.
Leaving home, eking out a livelihood in the
cities, accepting discouragement and rebuff,
undeterred by lovers or even by love itself,
she comes through at last to a success whose
chief reward is less in gold or plaudits than in
the sense of fidelity to her own high purpose.

In the end she has learned of "the inevitable hardness of human life," but also of the
richness of reward that comes with real creation. And in the end, too, she realizes the
lesson once more of the old German that
nothing is far and nothing is near; for, with
the world at her feet, she discovers that it
was potentially hers when she first set out
from her home town with her little legacy.
"I shall always measure things by that six
hundred dollars, just as I measure high buildings by the Moonstone standpipe." "There
is no work of art so big that it was not
once all contained in some youthful body."
"Art is only a way of remembering youth."

In *My Ántonia* (An-ton-ee'-ah) Miss Cather is not so kind to her heroine, at least in terms of material reward. Ántonia Shimerda is a Bohemian immigrant child of less than mediocre parentage, whose sole inheritance is a wholesome, hearty, clear-eyed courage. Brought up in the uses of adversity, she finds but one thing to which she can give a natural response; and that is, among the people of her own sort, "a kind of hearty joviality, a relish of life, not over-delicate, but very invigorating." This flourishes only among the folk who are held in despite by the respectables of the community. The dominant element are spiritually akin to the dominants of Spoon River and Gopher Prairie and Winesburg, Ohio, and to the selectmen of Friendship Village.

The life that went on in them seemed to me made up of evasions and negations; shifts to save washing and cleaning, devices to propitiate the tongue of gossip. This guarded mode of existence was like living under a tyranny. People's speech, their voices, their very glances, became furtive and repressed. Every individual taste, every natural appetite, was bridled by caution. The people asleep in their houses,

I thought, tried to live like the mice in their own kitchens; to make no noise, to leave no trace, to slip over the surface of things in the dark. The growing piles of ashes and cinders in the backyards were the only evidence that the wasteful, consuming process of life went on at all.

Ántonia has no spark of creative artistry; yet she feels the artist's desire to live a full, free life. She falls in love with a cheap seducer, and is abandoned on what she thinks is to be her honeymoon to become a mother without benefit of clergy. Later she marries a good, dull man, brings up a big family, and in the play of her native courage finds a very homely and very old-fashioned fulfilment of life. "That is happiness—to be dissolved in something complete and great." The greatness of Ántonia's achievement lies in the completeness of her dedication to her task—no less complete than that of Thea Kronburg. In Ántonia's contented domesticity Miss Cather offers a modern variation on an old theme. In the pages of Mrs. Stowe the latter stages of Ántonia's career would have been treated as steps of abnegation, the surrender to a sense of duty in a home on earth which would be rewarded by a mansion prepared on high. By most contemporary novelists it would be treated as a complete defeat, with no compensation either here or hereafter. But Miss Cather, with all her zest for studio life, has retained an imaginative regard for four walls and a hearthstone, and the vital experience of mothering a family.

After *My Ántonia* came a pause in Miss Cather's own story. *Youth and the Bright Medusa* is a kind of intermezzo of hesitancy between prairie land and Bohemia. Four of the short stories are reprinted from *The Troll Garden* of eight years earlier: a study in the temperament of a city-bred boy whose appetite for beauty and luxury lead him to theft, a week of nectar and ambrosia, and suicide; the overwhelming experience of a concert lover's first taste of music after a quarter-century of exile on the plains; the death in the far West of a consumptive singer who yearns to the end for the thrill and the glamor of her finest years; and the already-mentioned sculptor's funeral. The three purely exotic

stories of *The Troll Garden* were not reprinted.
It was the touch of the frontier that Miss
Cather chose to save. Yet, oddly enough,
the four new stories in the later volume have
none of this; all but one are wholly devoted
to the songstress in prosperity, and except
for that one they contribute but little to the
achievement of the author.

Evidently Miss Cather was not even yet
firmly established in the home of her imagination. As an artist she was attached to
the prairie stretches and the pioneer types,
but only in the half-sentimental fashion of
Ántonia's successful friend, James Burden,
who had gone out from obscurity into the
world of men and affairs, and in his strivings
and thrivings looked back with an affectionate sympathy which expressed itself in an
occasional hurried visit to the old neighborhood. He had outgrown it, like his youth;
and, like his youth, it symbolized to him "the
precious, the incommunicable past." In this
short-story intermezzo Miss Cather, sitting
in a New York apartment hotel, after a turn
around Washington Square, dealt with the

past tenderly and sympathetically, but as one who was evidently looking back toward it. She did not actually reawaken it as she had done before.

And so it is not surprising that in *One of Ours*, an aftermath of the war, Miss Cather allowed herself to be warped out of her own orbit, and that, as she swung through space in this flight, she vacillated between a life that she knew to the heart's core and a life of which she had only a remote and idealized conception. The boy who was "one of ours" belongs to the same countryside as do Alexandra and Thea and Ántonia. He is made restless by the same upwellings and outreachings of spirit, and, like his fellow-pioneers, is vaguely uncomfortable in the narrowness of the bed that he has not made for himself. A brutal accident, and gratitude to the woman who nurses him in his duress, horribly mismate him. The woman who is flung into his arms has shown her one pale gleam of warmth while he is prostrate and helpless. There is nothing in her to respond to ardor or even to affection. She is absorbed in her own chill righteousness which has been excelled in literature only by the centripetal goodness of that most obnoxiously virtuous woman, the Lady in *Comus*. Her final repudiation, in the name of the Lord, of every wifely obligation, sets him adrift just as America enters the war. Enlistment seems to offer him a hope of salvation. Fired with the fine zeal that inflamed the first thousands who responded to the call, he sets out on the crusade to save the world for democracy. Stupidity, sordidness, and chicane cannot overcome him. Reminders of the hollowness of his own lot cannot embitter him. In a final white heat of fervor he meets a glorious death on the battle-field.

It is a fine conception and it is rather thrillingly executed. It is doubtless true to what happened in the experience of some of the fallen; and in its heroic consummation it is certainly what those left to mourn would like to believe of every man who fell. Yet, on the whole, the romantic conception of war as a purifying fire belongs to the hopes of the new recruit and to the cherished recollections of the mourner. Now that the story of the war has been told, Philip Gibbs seems to be nearer the truth than Miss Cather. I have yet to find a soldier returned from overseas who has read the book without being stirred to protest at the concluding chapters of *One of Ours*. Barbusse and Dos Passos are more likely to be to their taste. They have been so far disillusioned that the death of the hero has seemed to them the snuffing of a candle rather than the apotheosis of a lover of democracy.

However far Miss Cather may have strayed from the paths in which she treads with a sure foot when she rambled into the latter part of *One of Ours*, she was at any rate not abandoning the theme of all her best work—the strife for self-fulfilment. Her soldier-boy-to-be begins his career in the frontier region of her three heroines. He encounters there the jealous leveling standards that would reduce all pioneers to jack-of-all-tradeship and general undistinction. And in his army career his restless spirit confronts conditions analogous to those that confront an artist in a philistine world. But in *A Lost Lady* Miss Cather loses her bearings altogether. The lost lady lives in the open West, and that is the only resemblance between her and the other major characters. Yet the distinction of the other characters is not that they live and work where pioneers or artists do, but that they have in them the stuff of which pioneers and artists are made: health, courage, a desire for freedom, a will to achieve. If they come through the conflict, their victories are worth winning. If they fail, their failures are tragic because they have the possibilities of victory in them. But the lost lady is a weakling and a ne'er-do-weel. She is a tarnished creature whose immorality lies not so much in the infraction of laws and precepts as in the fact that such a life as hers is inherently self-defeating. She is not even brilliantly alluring. The Elizabethans, with their sure word-usage, did well to call such a woman a "drab." Miss Cather's real creative work has been with really creative and colorful people.

These latter years have been disruptive and disconcerting. Miss Cather is one of many who seem to have been carried off their true courses by cross-winds and chop seas. Few of the men who have suffered this experience have even started back to port; most of those who have not foundered are hopelessly adrift. Yet one still hopes that this woman of clear observation and firm touch will find her way back to the elemental people whom she really knows. She was at her best when she was not distracted by the consciousness of current events or current problems. There are plenty of writers of less distinction to dabble with these. She may well return to her old ambition, and say once more of the prairie lands: *Primum ego in patriam mecum deducam Musam.*

BIOGRAPHICAL NOTE

Miss Cather was born at Winchester, Virginia, in 1876. The scant detail she has allowed to appear in *Who's Who* relates as the next fact that she was given her A.B. degree from the University of Nebraska in 1895. As her books recall nothing of Virginia and much of the plains, it is natural to believe that her

Willa Cather

impressionable years were spent in the West. From 1897 to 1901 she was on the staff of the *Pittsburgh Daily Leader*, and from 1906 to 1912 she was an assistant editor of *McClure's Magazine*. She lives in New York City.

Her books are: *April Twilights* (poems) 1903; *The Troll Garden*, 1905; *Alexander's Bridge*, 1912; *The Bohemian Girl*, 1912; *O Pioneers*, 1913; *The Song of the Lark*, 1915; *My Ántonia*, 1918; *Youth and the Bright Medusa*, 1920; *One of Ours*, 1922; *A Lost Lady*, 1923.

XI

The Short Story

NOT very long ago the expounders of America were saying that whatever else had been achieved in letters on this side the Atlantic—including in their "whatever" such negligible figures as Emerson, Whitman, and Mark Twain—the short story had at least been America's contribution to the literature of the world. There were Irving and Hawthorne and Poe, and Aldrich and Howells and James. And there was Richard Harding Davis and there were a hundred and fifty other people; and there was O. Henry. Whatever the Old World knew about the short story had been derived from Washington Irving or O. Henry, or the intervening writers. There was a chapter on the short story in every general history, articles regularly recurrent in the magazines, and books galore. Then about ten years ago there was an end to the to-do. There were no more books on the art or the theory or the technique of the short story. The drama came to the fore, and the books and articles were mostly on writing, staging, lighting, and producing plays. Now the stage is fighting to hold its own against poetry. Erato and Euterpe are making daily headway against Thalia and Melpomene, and books on the history, the theory, and the appreciation of poetry, and books on the pallid subject of versification serve as a counterpoint to the chorus of song that is issuing from the press. Yet all the while the short story, which has not any muse, continues blithely on its way. Colleges and correspondence schools conduct crowded courses, the best fruits of which are duly published. All the novelists, many of the dramatists, several of the essayists, and some of the poets write short stories in their moments of relaxation. The magazines are filled with them, the newspapers syndicate them, and every year E. J. O'Brien turns on his mechanical separator and dispenses the cream to the community in *The Best Short Stories of* ——.

The vital fact about the short story today is that the short story is what the public wants. Next to the news it is the most de-manded commodity in the market of printed goods; and it has even made itself a con-stant element in the newspapers—daily as well as Sunday. In the magazines literally hundreds are printed every month. The com-bined length of the Missouri-Mississippi is no more impressive than the river of printed narrative that is emptying itself into the gulf of oblivion. Some day the historian will turn to it for cultural signs of the times, and he will find signs as interesting and amusing as those that we now can find in the annuals—the Gems, and Keepsakes, and Amulets, and Offerings, the Tokens, and Caskets, and Leaf-lets of Memory—to which Poe and Haw-thorne were occasional contributors three generations ago.

When the technique of this type was being solemnly discussed a dozen or fifteen years back, the obvious special problems of concentration and rapidity of movement were stated over and over again. Let Bliss Perry speak for all the expositors of the short-story writer:

If his special theme be the delineation of character, he dare not choose colorless characters; if his theme is character-development, then that development must be hastened by striking experiences—like a plant forced in a hothouse instead of left to the natural conditions of sun and cloud and shower. For instance, if it be a love story, the hero and heroine must begin their decisive battle at once, without the advantage of a dozen chapters of preliminary skirmishing. If the hero is to be made into a villain or a saint, the chemistry must be of the swiftest; that is to say, unusual forces are brought to bear on somewhat unusual personalities.

But today the method of short-story telling has no longer the least appeal in itself. Cleverness in execution, valuable as it may be, is more or less taken for granted. Unusual forces and unusual personalities still rule, however, and the quest for subject-matter drives the ninety and nine in a far hunt for the things in heaven and earth that were not dreamed of in Horatio's philosophy. Most of them seem to be found in stories of the slum and immigrant, mystery stories, ghost stories—modern style—and exotic stories of adventure. The opening of "The Shame Dance," by W. D. Steele, is quite to the point:

"Stories of New York Life preferable." Well, then, here is a story of New York. . . . . It is a tale of this New York. That it didn't chance to happen in New York is beside the point. Where? It wouldn't help you much if I told you. Taai. That Island.

It doesn't.

The bulk of them is far too great to be compassed by any single reader who has anything else to do. There is no such process as selecting the best. Witness the testimony of the O. Henry Memorial Committee—five competent readers who at the end of 1921 picked five different stories as the best of that year, each one of which was so objected to by the remaining four that only one of them was even included in their composite list of sixteen. Yet a dozen volumes of collected narratives must include much of the good, and certainly much of the representative; and from these some safe deductions are possible.

The first outstanding fact is that, taken as a whole, the contemporary American short story fulfils a further comment of Mr. Perry's:

It is an interesting consequence of this necessity for choosing the exceptional rather than the normal that, so far as the character-element is concerned, the influence of the modern short story is thrown upon the side of romanticism rather than of realism.

In this respect there is the sharpest of contrasts between the output of today and that of a generation ago. From the Civil War to the end of the century the "local colorists" were in full career. The mining camp, Creole New Orleans, the Tennessee mountains, the plantation negro, the old Virginia families, the villagers of Pennsylvania, the metropolitans of Van Bibber's acquaintance, the coast and hill-town New Englanders, and the toilers of the mid-western wheat fields were developed in turn. The short story was as much of an innovation as the camera. Everybody was taking snapshots, and the chief point of interest at first was in picturing sectional traits and local conditions of life. The form itself was unusual, and the material of the stories, which were written for national magazine consumption, was unusual for all but the residents of the particular sections which supplied it.

Before the first charm of this sort of fiction was exhausted the concoction of clever ingenuities came into vogue. Aldrich developed the surprise ending with new effectiveness. Marjorie Daw, incomparable village maiden, turns out in the last sentence never to have existed except in the mind of a convalescent letter-writer; the acrobat, Mademoiselle Olympe Zabriski, proves to be a man; *A Struggle for Life* does not occur; *Two Bites at a Cherry* converts an apparent widow into a twice-married woman; *Her Dying Words* precede her rescue. There is a neat contour to all these stories, but never a suggestion of blood, bone, or sinew. The characters are like ivory chess men, and the man who manipulates them always contrives to end the game with a neat and unexpected move. Stockton, with his voluminous output—

The Short Story

standard edition, eighteen volumes—turned
the tables on the surprise ending with the
dilemma ending of *The Lady or the Tiger*, and
gave the rest of his work the stamp of whimsical extravaganza. He invented a negative
gravity, set a man to haunting his own ghost,
and, in the fashion attributed to American
humor, gravely accumulated circumstantial
detail around events that never happened on
land or sea. O. Henry was the latest inheritor
of the sheer-cleverness tradition. How far
past he already seems! That particular form
of unusualness has, for the time being, gone
the way of all the earth.

For one who knows contemporary literature mainly through books, the natural
inclination is to estimate the short story of
today by sizing up the products of the best-
known men and women now writing in
America. What could be more logical than
to depend on Garland, Dreiser, Tarkington,
Wharton, Cabell, Willa Cather, Hergesheimer, Anderson, for one's findings? Perhaps, in absolute terms, nothing could be;
but the awkward question will not down as

to whether these writers are actually the best known to the world of short-story readers. As a matter of fact, they are not. I look in a half-dozen books of collected narrative within arm's reach and in a half-dozen magazines, and find that five stories out of one hundred and twenty-six are by these "best-known" authors. The short-story world is a periodical world with its own hall of fame. It has its own marks of distinction, too. If one were to draw deductions from the eight writers in my list above, and to speculate on probabilities in short-storydom, it would be natural to expect a rather drastic realism in current narrative. What will be the obvious aftermath of the Spoon River, Winesburg, Gopher Prairie crop? Yet in the run of the stories the element of realism is slight. What Mr. Perry wrote twenty years ago is still true; they fall on the romantic side of the scale.

In these stories the lot of the immigrant is the fulfilment of hopes for the promised land. Two fugitives from Russian pogroms realize that they are in Paradise when a New

The Short Story

York traffic policeman holds up motor cars for five blocks on either side to let them cross the street. Liberty, fraternity, equality! An East Side Jewish boy at twenty becomes world-famed as a violinist, and enlists for the Great War. Another Jew, circulation manager for a New York daily, befriends a broken-down Englishman and rises to fine heights of magnanimity when his charge turns ingrate. A man is always a man, in any guise. A down-and-outer who picks up small change by pretending epilepsy to outpouring theater crowds refuses a substantial bribe rather than hurt a woman's feelings. They are the same sentimental stuff out of which Bret Harte fabricated the saints and heroes of Poker Flat and Roaring Camp. The realism of hardship as hardship rarely appears in these creations—the sort of thing that Stephen Crane did twenty-five years ago. And the immigrant in the laboring world is seldom to be found in narrative. He aspires finely, but he toils not, neither does he spin. Myra Kelly was the last to draw consistently truthful pictures of this sort.

However, the resort of the short-story world to romance is by no means to be wholly attributed to the limitations of the type— "The consequence of the need for choosing the exceptional rather than the normal." A public demand is the real determinant. Here is a magazine known to everybody, with an immense circulation, and an income mainly derived from its advertisers. The chief advertisements in the copy at hand are a cosmetic, a shaving soap, a chewing gum, a tooth paste, a system of fat reduction, a correction for bow legs and knock knees, a nose-shaper, a hair-restorer, a cheap candy, diamonds-on-the-instalment (two), and get-rich-quick correspondence courses (five). The people who buy those commodities are going to buy the sort of stories that go with them. That is clear enough. And it is as clear as a bow leg or a crooked nose that the people who want these commodities are not likely to be either very analytical or very imaginative. They want thrills and "a punch"; and they want these things as avidly as they want beauty in their own bodies.

The Short Story

The same impulse that makes them shrink from gray hairs, wrinkles, and increasing girth makes them rejoice in escape from actuality in their fiction. And the same credulity that makes them believe they can become expert salesmen, artists, and authors "in twenty lessons" Lodgically subjects them to the spell of the up-to-date ghost story.

To make quite sure I run once more over the contents of four volumes of collected narratives. One-fifth of them are in the undiscovered country—on the borders of ghostland—and half the remainder are in the realm of Somewhere Else, in the "North Country," in Biskra, Kairwan, Taai, vaguely in India, at Port au Prince and Point au Fer. Look them up if you choose in your atlas. (But you won't.) One gets the feeling that perhaps some of the writers have been at the places described, but that certainly most of them have not. In these remote spots picturesque and often desperate men and women are involved in picturesque and desperate experiences. But they are almost all stage figures with visible make-ups playing against wobbly scenery. As Mr. Steele says, it is beside the point that the events did not happen in New York, or better, in the moving-picture studios of Hollywood. It is beside the point not only because they never happened at all, but because the code of New York could never have been imposed on people who never were subjected to it. French Eva on Naapu commits suicide because a Chinaman whispers to an American ship-chandler that there is a touch of black blood in her veins. Yet even "the magnates of Naapu were a multicolored lot." In the case of Konrad Berkovici, who presumably has been to the home of his memory in his Roumanian tales, another complication quite as baffling taxes the reader: a difference of standards so great that it cannot be overleaped. Ghitza, pride of his gypsy nation, wrestles with a Tartar champion for a stake that means riches or poverty for all his people. On the brink of defeat, he breaks away and makes his escape. Strangely enough "all bets are off." "Of all the great heroes, why is it that Ghitza has not been given the place of honor?" What is the use of even answering such a query? Sometimes again the story defies any conceivable human test. An Italian lady of quality is rapt away by the conqueror of her own people. She is compact of all most delicate qualities; he is a ravishing brute. She hates him to begin with, and loathes him beyond expression when she suspects him of having flayed a lover of hers, and of disporting a vest made from his soft skin. She discovers that he has not committed this indelicacy and straightway loves him. Now, really. . . . .

Fiction from the outset has had its recurrent waves of interest in supernaturalism, coming at intervals of about a generation. The after-effects of the Great War have heightened the emphasis on spirits and spiritism, as have the vagaries of Lodge and Doyle —Sir Oliver and Sir Arthur. Possibly because such material is elusive, and stories dealing with it must needs be well handled to be readable at all, these most incredible of tales average far higher in execution than the romances of physical event. A man happily remarried broods on the memory of his first wife, and brings her visibly back to other members of his household. A commonplace city youth has a dire illness, after which he is from time to time "possessed" with powers overwhelming to all within his presence. A gardener's son, dumb and "queer," seems to be a spiritual part of the plant-world. He is educated, and, developing into a natural scientist, deplores the loss of certain instinctive wisdom that he cannot put into words. It is the "Intimations of Immortality" theme. There is a thrill as well as a thought in many of these stories—the best of them. And there is always a fascination about them, even when as in two cases the heroes have to be persuaded that they are dead. In the general field of heightened romance—the romance of adventure, not of the spirit-world—Wilbur Daniel Steele seems to be the most consistent workman. He is selected for honors by every compiler and very properly. He has a technique and a feeling for his characters which makes them behave credibly, and he lures his readers successfully away from the world of circumstance.

There is a residuum of stories about actual American life, perhaps one-fourth of the whole number. They are of every substance and every construction, the more genially amusing by L. H. Robbins and Thomas Beer, the deftly analytical by Susan Glaspell and Mrs. Gerould (when she stays at home for her material), and the most substantially American in texture and treatment by Fannie Hurst (and we would say Edna Ferber if she were in the anthologies. Is it copyright that holds her out?). These are told each in its own way. The Sherwood Anderson contributions are sketches—not stories in any technical sense. There is a tabloiding of the whole content of Spoon River, done in fresh terms and called *The Life of Five Points*, which is quite worth reprinting, but which is a short story only by the most liberal construction. This residuum is all very interesting and all very chaotic, like the American life from which it is derived.

The whole territory is much too extensive
and diverse for neatly conclusive dogma-
tisms; but I am tempted to two general
observations, or a single observation in two
parts. The short story in America today is
the literary form which is addressed to and
read by the nation as a whole. It reaches
literally millions and it reaches them through
magazines. It therefore answers to a public
demand, and the public is never in the position of feverishly demanding intellectual
stimulants. The most that it will ask for—
it will accept more, but that is a different
matter—the most that it will ever *ask* for is
something that may awake emotional and
moral reactions, thrills, and good resolutions
that do not last too long. And the public
that swarm to the "movies" and to Messrs.
Bryan and Sunday get scores upon scores of
stories every month, mostly of the kind that
they want, and some of them very excellent
of their kind.

In the meanwhile, the incorrigible pen-
men who are more interested in life and in
artistry than they are in sales go on in their

own way, their work appearing in the books which are read by only a small fraction of the periodical buyers; and their work should be considered in quite a different light. They write much more about America, and they think infinitely more about it. They are consciously trying to see life in this country, and to interpret it in their own native ways. It is a great chaos, so that their writing about it is at once bold and tentative. But while the purveyors of popular thrills are testifying to an existing public, these recorders of life are speculating about a potential nation, and we do not begin an approach to the whole truth unless we take both elements into account. Mr. O'Brien's last Preface has one suggestive point. Although he fails to discriminate explicitly between the two kinds, he significantly uses the word "book," you will notice:

I suggested, moreover, that from the point of view of the great artist these books were all more or less magnificent failures which were creating, little by little, out of the shock of conflict an ultimate harmony, out of which the great book for which we are all waiting in America might come, ten years from now, or five years, or even tomorrow.

The orchestra is tuning up.

BIBLIOGRAPHY

Among the short-story collections the following are representative:

Heydrick, B. A. *Americans All*. Harcourt, Brace, 1920.

Howells, W. D. *Great Modern American Stories*. Boni and Liveright, 1920.

Jessop, Alexander. *Representative American Short Stories*. Allyn and Bacon, 1923.

Laselle, M. A. *Short Stories of the New America*. Holt, 1919.

Law, F. H. *Modern Short Stories*. Century, 1918.

O'Brien, E. J. H. *Best Short Stories for 1915*, etc. Published annually. Small, Maynard.

Pence, R. W. *Short Stories by Present Day Authors*. Macmillan, 1912.

Thomas, C. S. *Atlantic Narratives*, 2 vols. Atlantic, 1918, 1921.

Wick, Jean. *The Editors Buy and Why*. Small, Maynard, 1921.

Williams, B. C. *Our Short Story Writers*. Moffat, Yard, 1920.

Williams, B. C. *O. Henry Memorial Award Prize Stories of 1921*. Doubleday, Page, 1922.

XII

The Drift of the Drama

THE things that are taking place on the American stage and with the American drama today are logical developments from the beginnings in this country; for, from the first, there has been a regular progression, slow but unbroken, toward independent management, fresh technique, home-bred acting, and the use of native material.

For a round hundred years and more, the control of the theater was in the hands of British-born managers, the chief playing was done by imported actors, and the plays were naturally what the producers and actors brought with them. When William Dunlap (1766–1839) and John Howard Payne (1795–1852), native Americans, broke into the limelight they changed affairs but little. Dunlap applauded himself for writing on

American themes; but he actually abandoned English models for German ones, doing his most distinctive work as translator and adapter of Kötzebue, Schiller, and Zschokke. And at the same time Payne, who found nothing to write about at home, was equally docile in his pursuit of French models. Edwin Forrest in the 1830's made an interesting attempt to encourage American writing, especially on primitive American life, but of the nine prize plays that he secured, the very earliest dried up the native spring of material and the rest depended on primitiveness as embodied in the primitive emotions of highly civilized types, of whom Spartacus was the most famous, and the Broker of Bogota one of the most impressive.

Taken by and large, the nineteenth century contributed no distinguished American playwrights. The names that stand out in stage history are the names of controlling managers, men of British parentage like the Wallacks and Augustin Daly, or of players of foreign descent like the Jeffersons, the Booths, the Hacketts, and the Sotherns;

and the writers of plays, encouraged by stage demands rather than by literary conditions, were the theatrical successors of Dunlap and Payne—like Dion Boucicault with his 124 plays, and Bronson Howard with his less numerous but no more distinguished array of stage successes. But at last, well toward 1900, there began to win recognition a new generation of playwrights who knew drama in its relation to the other arts and who wrought with it as literature, even though they were not indifferent to box-office returns as no genuine dramatist is.

The movement started in England and on the Continent and, as we can now see, in America as well, though the traditional American neglect of American literature led the first alert critics on this side the Atlantic to lay all their emphasis on European innovators. As a matter of fact, the best contemporary plays that reached the stage did come from across the water. By 1910, however, the drift of things was suggested in the contents of Walter Pritchard Eaton's *At the New Theater and Others*. In this book, of twenty-three plays reviewed, ten were by Americans, two of the chief essay subjects were Clyde Fitch and William Winter, and the dedication of the volume is most significant of all. For it gave due credit to Professor George P. Baker, of Harvard, as "Founder in that institution of a pioneer course for the study of dramatic composition" and as "inspiring leader in the movement for a better appreciation among educated men of the art of the practical theater." With this movement a new audience and a new drama began developing together, and a generation of playwrights gave over the imitation and adaptation of French and German plays, returned to American dramatic material, and achieved results that are readable as well as actable. The business man continued in control of the amusement world, but he began to be aware that that world contained an element of discriminating and thoughtful people.

When Professor Baker at Harvard and Professor Matthews at Columbia began to divide their attention between the older and the modern drama, they were looked at by some with wonder and by others with amused skepticism. Yet before long their students became not only intelligent theater-goers but contributors as critics and playwrights to the literature of the stage. And then, in the natural order of events, the whole student body came to realize that the older drama should both be reduced to its proper place and restored to it; that it was an interesting chapter in literary and social history because it was not a closed chapter, but a preliminary to the facts of the present.

The most ambitious recent attempt to put the play on the same plane with the symphony and the orchestra, which are always liberally subsidized, was the experiment of the celebrated and short-lived New Theater in New York from 1909 to 1911. That it failed within two years is not half so important as that it was founded, that others on smaller scales were also founded and failed, that municipal theaters sprang up here and there and were supported according to various plans, that producers like Winthrop

Ames and Stuart Walker became established in popular favor, that the Drama League of America spread its influence over the whole country, that the printing of plays and collections of plays rose to an unprecedented output, that scores on scores of little theaters, neighborhood theaters, and peoples' country theaters were founded. There are two main fruits of all this soil preparation and seeding: One, that in the production and staging of plays the attempts of the experimenters to appeal to the imagination in devices of stage lighting and setting have often been approved and adopted by the regents of the commercial theater; and the other, that in the career of the Theater Guild of New York the production of the best literary plays in the best dramatic manner has been rewarded with a series of popular successes almost without parallel in this country. The Napoleonic theatrical managers are still in the saddle, but the uncommercial stage is coming to be more important every season. The leaven of popular intelligence is at work. The seasons of 1923–25 were the most brilliant and substantial, as far as plays go, in the history of the American stage.

The progress and the changes that have taken place within recent years in lighting, setting, and costuming plays, have more to do with the nature of plays to be written than appears at first glance. When Augustus Thomas came along with his "plays of States" in the early nineties, and Clyde Fitch with his social satires and comedies, simple literal settings were all that were needed, and they were conscientiously provided. But when the demands of such plays as *Peer Gynt* and *Chanticleer* and *The Blue Bird* showed how little could be achieved with the conventional devices, fresh inventiveness was set to work. And if necessity was the mother of invention in the metropolitan theaters, it was so with a double reason in all the little theaters which had immense ambitions, no capital, and scant revenue. The realistic setting, which is totally inadequate for the farther reaches of imaginative drama, proved also to be too expensive for use in successions of plays which needed different interiors and out-of-door scenes, particularly for little theaters using three or four one-act plays in a single program. So the sky dome, and the cyclorama, and the interchangeable unit set, and the employment of lighting—and shadowing—were all called upon to suggest both the utterly elusive and the relentlessly obvious. Scouted at first by Belasco and his school, they were found to be effective and beautiful as well as economical.

The results have been many and striking. Thus lately while Warfield was playing Shylock against a background of scrupulously faithful detail, Barrymore did his hundred and one Hamlet performances with the simplest and most impressive of modern settings. The Kennedys in *The Chastening* suggested all outdoors by a glimpse through curtains of a back drop that may have been 10 feet wide, but looked hardly more than half that. And these modern settings have done another unattempted thing. In addition to stimulating the imaginations of audiences to reach beyond anything that paint

and canvas could indicate, they have gone
in the other direction to suggest the poverty
or the pathology of the imaginations of stage
characters by presenting the bleak fancies of
thwarted and inelastic minds—like the glar-
ing stupidity of the courtroom in Liliom's
heaven, or the maddening unrelief of the
counting-room in *The Adding Machine*, where
Mr. Zero finally does go mad, and where, instead of the murder he commits, a picture of
his murderous mind is actually staged.

It could hardly come about that development of a new-tempered theater audience,
and the elaboration of new ways of gaining
stage effects, would take place without any
appreciable change in the plays themselves,
especially in a time of such general artistic
experimentation as the present. There have
been many innovations, as they are usually
called, though anyone with a historical
sense knows that such apparent novelties
are more often than not old and unfamiliar
as well as new and strange. One has only to
go back far enough, for instance, to find a
time before English and continental drama

were affected by classical models and to come to legitimate predecessors of the modern type that disregards division of plays into acts, and builds them out of successions of variously numerous scenes. We have to go no farther than the two plays already mentioned, *Liliom* and *The Adding Machine*, to meet with just such structure in the present.

It has been generally considered, again, that the soliloquy was an abandoned dramatic device. People do not talk aloud alone in actual life, it was said, and therefore they should not be required to in dramatic portrayal. It would not be hard to list by the hundred plays of recent authorship in which there is no soliloquy and no aside. A few notable exceptions could be cited, and in these it could be shown that the soliloquies are no longer clumsy dramatic expedients for bridging gaps in dialogue, but genuine dramatic units, equivalents for whole passages of dialogue, dramatic substitutes for what the novelist does unchallenged when he analyzes or narrates the mental and emotional experiences of characters who may be quite

passive in body. The most striking example
of this method of "exposition" is evidently
The Emperor Jones, which is presented in eight
scenes, of which all but the first and last are
carried by a single speaker. The crumbling
of the boastful negro, the breakdown of confidence, and the upwelling of a host of
fears is remorselessly pursued by soliloquy,
and visualized in the imaginative settings
and pantomimic figures which represent not
characters at all, but phantasms of a disor-
dered mind. If this can be successfully done,
it stands to reason that other experiments
would follow in the use of castes of two or
three; and they have, on various themes from
Henry Myers' *The First Fifty Years* to Charles
Rann Kennedy's *The Chastening*.

When we come to the outstanding character of the plays, detached from questions
and effects of production, the feature that
challenges attention first is the proportion
of plays that appeal rather more to the intellect than to the emotions. Of course there is
no denying the vogue of the mystery play.
The Bat flew its mysterious and baffling

course, and was followed across the stage by an arkful of cats and mice and canaries and crooks and foreign adventuresses and what Penrod called "deteckatives" armed with "revolavers" and flash-lights and general obtuseness. But it is an interesting commentary on the public appetite for villains and swashbucklers that *Captain Applejack* flourished as it did; for the whole point of this amusing play is to turn to gentle scorn a specious hankering for the thrillers of the Spanish Main and the hair-raising possibilities of the country-house. People chuckled through this comedy with one eye on the stage and the other on the play of their own emotions, getting quite half their fun from the analysis of their theatrical gullibility. It is only such a public which could conceivably have carried *Six Characters in Search of an Author* through three months of a New York season, for this is nothing more than an essay on dramatic theory interpreted through dialogue and action.

It is characteristic of the period that so many actable plays have been presented on the generally unromantic theme, "And so they did not live happily ever after." It is an inevitable effect of the contemporary acknowledgment that not all marriages are made in heaven, and in harmony with the same minor strain in scores of novels. Of the various approaches to the subject Miss Akins' *Déclassée*, Mr. Richman's *Ambush*, and Miss Glaspell's *The Verge* have been among the most successful. Mr. Jesse Lynch Williams has written on the theme most merrily in *Why Marry?* and *Why Not?;* and Miss Rachel Crothers has persisted most seriously in presenting the woman's answers to both questions in *The Three of Us*, *A Man's World*, *He and She*, *Nice People*, and many others. Mr. Williams' attitude is perhaps more balanced than Miss Crothers'; for he believes, very sensibly, that however much of general readjustment there may be in the contemporary social world, the adjustment that will provide the foundations of marriage is and always will be the mutual tolerance and the mutual fair play without which no two humans can long live at close range, whether in or out of matrimony. It is not a profound conclusion, but it is sensible; and the dramatic presentation of common sense, filled with incident and spiced with wise humor, is likely to make good plays and good literature. Witness the Kaufmann-Connolly *Dulcy* and *To the Ladies*, which are complete fulfilments of this formula. It is reassuring in the latter of these comedies to find the wise woman who can survive the discovery—or the conviction—that she has a better head than her husband's. Life is full of them. Very few of them have found their way happily on to the stage.

There is a rather striking contrast offered between the wild reaches of romantic material explored in the short stories of the day and the homely backgrounds of most of the plays. The big city is behind a great many of them, though it is seldom featured in any spectacular way. The more serious human studies are in the smaller places, and parallel the stories of the village or of the revolt from the village that figure so largely in the contemporary novel. Some of these are dramatized novels, as in the cases of the successful *Miss Lulu Bett* and the ineffectual *Main Street*. They deal with the Middle West, as also in Berger's *The Deluge*, the Carolina mountains, as in Miss Kummer's *The Mountain Man*, or the old South, as in A. E. Thomas' *Just Suppose*. New material is being all the time developed in the people's country theaters in North Dakota and North Carolina; and the publication of the *Carolina Plays* will perhaps spread the field of their presentation beyond their native state. But next in importance to the Theater Guild of New York in the world of the uncommercial theater, and most important of all the local centers of production are the Provincetown Players, with their successive publications, and a membership that includes such creative writers as Floyd Dell, Alfred Kreymborg, George Cram Cook, Susan Glaspell, and Eugene O'Neill.

Sooner or later any discussion of the American play must come around to Eugene O'Neill; and he is fitting playwright to conclude a sketch with, because he is the preeminent one of the moment, and because in him and his career so much of recent American theatrical and dramatic history are combined. The son of a popular actor, he was bred in the atmosphere of the theater. After a conventional schooling and an abbreviated college experience, he had four years on the sea and at the far ports that sea life reaches. And the lure of the sea is written into his works just as is his subsequent invalidism. From 1913 on, he has been recording himself in playwriting. He had his turn as many another has with Professor Baker at Harvard, and he joined the little-theater brigade as the most distinguished member of the Provincetown Players.

It is almost too logical an evolution that the outstanding contributor to dramatic literature in this country during the last five seasons should be the son of an old-school actor, the pupil of the new-school teacher of dramatic technique, a representative of the independent peoples' theater movement, and a successful user of native material. Yet these facts are combined in Mr. O'Neill. There were several years of 'prenticeship before he reached the larger audience of New York and the beyond to which New York successes are taken; but in 1919–20 he made his mark with *Beyond the Horizon;* in the next season came *The Emperor Jones* and *Diff'rent;* in 1921–22, *The Straw, Anna Christie, The Hairy Ape,* and *The First Man;* and in the next season two of these were repeated. Of these, *Beyond the Horizon* and *Anna Christie* were awarded the Pulitzer prizes for being the best American plays of their respective years, and *The Hairy Ape* was selected in 1922 as the most egregious American play for presentation at the Odéon in Paris. *Welded* and *All God's Chillun's Got Wings* were the productions of early 1924.

In selecting the material for these plays, O'Neill has made no slightest concession to the popular liking for glad and sunny stuff. In handling this material it is alleged that he has sometimes yielded a bit in connection with his play endings. Yet even here the surrender has been only partial. On the whole, he presents a grim life in a grim way. His first success is a study of decadence and defeat in the New England that made the material for Miss Wilkins' *Pembroke* and Mrs. Wharton's *Ethan Frome*. *Straw* is a play of spiritual triumph for a consumptive victim; *Anna Christie*, a chronicle of regeneration, though a picture of the most sordid conditions; *The Hairy Ape*, a study in human isolation told from the point of view of a steamship stoker. A play by O'Neill is the last possible resort for the matinée girl or the tired business man. But O'Neill has achieved his audience without regard to them. He deals with fundamental human emotions and experiences, he presents conditions faithfully, dodging none of the essential but unpleasant facts, and beneath all he shows an admiration for and a faith in the virtues of endurance and integrity. It is a fact not to be underestimated that the American public—not merely the critics—are all attention when he chooses to speak.

The Drift of the Drama

BIBLIOGRAPHY

GENERAL DISCUSSIONS

Burleigh, Louise. *The Community Theatre*, 1917.

Burton, Richard. *The New American Drama*, 1913.

Cheney, Sheldon. *The New Movement in the Theater*, 1914; *The Art Theater*, 1917.

Clark, B. H. *The British and American Drama of Today*, 1915.

Dickinson, T. H. *The Case of American Drama*, 1915; *The Insurgent Theater*, 1917.

Eaton, W. P. *The American Stage of Today*, 1908; *At the New Theater and Others*, 1910.

MacKaye, Percy. *The Playhouse and the Play*, 1909; *The Civic Theater*, 1912.

COLLECTIONS OF PLAYS

Baker, George P. *Modern American Plays*, 1920.

Moses, M. J. *Representative Plays by American Dramatists*, Vol. III, 1921.

Quinn, A. H. *Representative American Plays*, 1917; *Contemporary American Plays*, 1923.

XIII

Bostonia and Bohemia

I

"WHEN we get back," William James wrote to an old friend in 1900, "we must see each other daily, and may the days of both of us be right long in the State of Massachusetts! Bless her!" It was an amiable confirmation of Holmes's comment forty years earlier: "Boston Statehouse is the Hub of the Solar System. You couldn't pry that out of a Boston man if you had the tire of all creation straightened out for a crowbar."

In the place called Boston today there are very few genuine Bostonians. Most of those who consider themselves as such are like Aldrich, but not as candid as he was when he confessed that he was not really Boston— only Boston-plated. The real Frogpondian must trace back—like Emerson's Concord roster—Bulkeley, Hunt, Willard, Hosmer, Meriam, Flint—unchallenged to the seventeenth century. That is why William James was almost presumptuous in speaking so fervently of Beacon Hill and its dependencies; and why Henry Adams could be considered hardly more than an adopted son before he became a prodigal. (My deah! Before *John* Adams, who ever heard of the family? And as for *his* social position! Well, really—.") There are, however, some few scions of the "Mayflower" who really belong to the place, and whose actions truly smack of the soil.

One is baffled to say just what is the root difference between Boston and Philadelphia. The clever bromides about the surviving traditions and all that are interchangeable. Yet, somehow, the Boston tradition seems to have been mainly centripetal, while Philadelphia seems to have tossed off more coruscations to the outer world. At any rate, against the many Bostonians of stable single-mindedness, Philadelphia offered as many examples of facile versatility. This is what John Adams himself recognized when he wrote back from the Continental Congress to Mistress Abigail (whose mother was a Quincy):

> I met Mr. Francis Hopkinson. . . . . He is one of your pretty little, curious, ingenious men. . . . . I wish I had leisure and tranquillity of mind to amuse myself with those elegant and ingenious arts of painting, sculpture, statuary, architecture, and music. But I have not.

And it is this same contrast that nearly a hundred and fifty years later is suggested by the posthumous volumes of Thomas Wentworth Higginson and James Gibbons Huneker.

Mr. Higginson was born in Boston in 1823, played with little James Lowell, went to Harvard, preached himself out of orthodoxy, joined the antislavery forces, backed John Brown, headed a negro regiment in the Civil War, and had a hand in the early numbers of the *Atlantic*. He wrote books on American history and literature, on *Common Sense about Women*, on *Old Cambridge* and *Cheerful Yesterdays* and *Contemporaries* and *Carlyle's Laugh*, and did lives of Whittier and

Longfellow and Margaret Fuller. He knew
Arnold and the Brownings and Fitzgerald
and Sainte-Beuve and Stepniak. He read dispassionately. He edited the poems of Emily
Dickinson, and ignored Whitman. He lived
broadly a life of affairs, but he was a local
man, in the best sense a hearty provincial, a
fit representative of Bostonia.

Mr. Huneker was born in Philadelphia
in 1860, his grandfather an Irish poet, his
father a musician. He passed by way of a
military and a law school to ten years as
student and teacher of piano. He enjoyed
much residence and frequent travel abroad,
though for the last thirty years until his
death in 1921 he was a New York journalist,
writing on music, the drama, and painting.
One of his favorite phrases became the title
of the *Seven Arts Magazine*. He wrote on
Chopin and Liszt, on the modern European
dramatists in *Iconoclasts*, and the painters in
Promenades of an Impressionist; on New York
in *The New Cosmopolis;* on whatever he chose
to in *Ivory Apes and Peacocks* and *Unicorns*
and *Bedouins;* and on himself in *Steeplejack*

(two volumes). He knew George Moore and Joseph Conrad and Antonin Dvořák and Bernard Shaw and Caruso. He read omnivorously, and everything he wrote was a palimpsest on which the traces of his reading were apparent. He delighted in Flaubert and Verlaine, and had recovered bravely from Whitmania. He was a cosmopolitan of the sidewalks, and to the end of his life a boyishly naughty Bohemian.

Mr. Higginson in his declining years published *Part of a Man's Life*, and Mr. Huneker gave out his autobiography just before his sudden death. Posthumously there appeared Higginson's *Letters and Journals*, culled from all along his life, and Huneker's last journalistic articles—*Variations* and his *Letters*. We could easily dispense with the autobiographies.

It would hardly be fair to judge Colonel Higginson by what he issued at eighty-two. In addition to local reminiscences (the gist of which is in earlier volumes), he wrote on children's sayings, on butterflies in poetry (the real, winged things, not ephemeral poets), on little-read books (praising a man who had read Gibbon four times), and on the close of the Victorian epoch. Only one chapter out of the fourteen seems to have been written because he really wanted to say something: "The Cowardice of Culture," which decries the cheap pessimism of the perennial calamity-wailer. In the rest of the book he figures as the venerable talker whose distinction obliges his listeners to conceal incipient yawns.

Mr. Huneker's much-heralded *Steeplejack* is no better in its way, and it would be less than charitable to judge him by it. Thirty years in the opera-house, the theater, the concert halls, and the art galleries, with thirty years of intimate conversation and professional interviewing and cormorant reading and eating and drinking, might have marshaled for us a rather splendid pageant of the arts. Instead, we are taken into the side streets, where we get little except a vague impression from out of the beery, shrill-voiced confusion—Dvořák with his nineteenth cocktail, De Pachmann fiercely demanding his cognac, Agnani drunk, and big nights when the celebrants were brought home in the cold, gray dawn, under the pilotage of benevolent cabbies. We are dining with a gourmand rather than with an epicure.

II

The two posthumous volumes are more substantial. From Colonel Higginson's journals we get a view of a stalwart optimist in the midst of a substantial community. At twenty-five he was challenging the leaders of his denomination in open convention. "I told them that the one thing that interested us (younger men) in them was the capacity we saw in them of being better than they were." Soon he was on cordial terms with Professor Crosby. "He has a taste for heretics, and comes to see me constantly." At thirty-eight, according to his own account, he was a tolerantly amused pariah in Cambridge. He was an eclectic liberal, very conscious of the difference between himself and the miscellaneous "come-outers" who cheered for everything new on general prin-

ciples. At forty-three he alluded to an Eng-
lishwoman as "very radical" because she
wished women to vote and be physicians,
and a year or two later he described Albert
Dicey and James Bryce in the same terms.
Another young man to whom he gave more
space was later to share diplomatic honors
with Mr. Bryce. Here is a description of a
military picnic which was "got up" for a
young Mr. Hay, President Lincoln's private
secretary:

. . . . A nice young fellow, who unfortunately
looks about seventeen, and is oppressed with the
necessity of behaving like seventy. . . . . About four
came the band, the officers, the young ladies, General Saxton without his livelier half, Mr. Hay laboring
not to appear newmown.

Higginson's humor was always pleasantly
unforced, as when he wrote of Philadelphia
that he had been to the opera and then home
with "the Petersons, who have $100,000 a
year from *Peterson's Magazine*, and horrify
the ancient Philadelphia families by the
good taste with which they spend their
money."

Mr. Higginson's breeding was far more distinguished than his culture—or "cultivation" as he preferred to call it. In ethics, as in etiquette, he had the sort of impeccability that seems rather to be born of natural balance than of self-control. Of beauty he was as abstinent as Thoreau was of his material things. He liked literary men, but had no passion for books; as for the other arts, if his pages were to be the sole evidence of them, the evidence would be nil. He revealed at times a happy gift of phrase, but no style or even stylisms. He was a thoroughly Saturday-clubbish manner of man, good-humored, cheerful, self-contained, capable of a good fight, though anything but pugnacious, and withal a conscious and reasoned optimist.

III

Mr. Huneker's *Variations*, a miscellany of essaylets on the arts written toward the end of his life, nevertheless is still the work of a jolly youngster at play, an abounding individual who loved persons and personalities, and was a personality himself. He cared

more for conditions than for theories; principles were of little interest to him, but the
applications of principles were all engrossing.
He loved talk for its own sake, and was much
given to monologue. Like that great but
unrecognized genius, Captain Craig, Huneker
would not have been Huneker without his
verbosity. Yet *Variations* subtracted little
from the disappointment of *Steeplejack*. The
Bohemian self-consciousness in both books is
the reason for their flatness. It is a bore to
sit long with people who talk as if a glass of
beer were an adventure, and a mild jag a
modest accomplishment.

It is the absence of such self-consciousness that makes the *Letters* which followed
so much more genuine and readable than the
story he chose to give to the world a year or
two before his death. The boyishness that
made him say in *Variations* that Bernard
Shaw probably thought of him as a "pie-
eyed youth who was all roses and raptures"
is obvious enough in his notes and letters to
his friends; but it is boyhood unaware of
itself, not showing off. He writes to an

editor: "I promise that if you will allow me
to call and say good-bye to you the week of
August first some afternoon, I shall not talk
so much as I have done in this letter. I feel
quite hoarse." To an editor: "I think it is a
better book. But better or not it's the last
I'll ever write on fantastic, exotic, erotic,
esoteric, idiotic themes. I'm done. . . . ."
To a fellow-author: "I enjoyed the 'Pal.'
Print it somewhere simply to make someone
mad. *That's* a sweet joy, too." And to a
critic, after a painful accident in Cologne:
"Hell and Hominy! But I hate work after
three months' loafing (and my ribs in a
sling)."

He was versatile with the uncalculating
enthusiasm of a boy who will turn from one
hilltop to another with complete disregard
for all the hard climbing it involves. It's
the fresh view he was after. Yet he realized
how extravagant he was of effort, writing
to a friendly critic: "Of course, you saw
through the elbow-grease versatility paragraph. All the work in the world won't
produce versatility—and I'm sorry to add

that versatility too often spells superficial-
ity." Yet five years later, in 1912, he wrote
of one month's travel:

I've interviewed Lloyd George (*New York World*),
Joseph Conrad (*Times*), Matisse (*Times*), the Futurists
(*Metropolitan Magazine*), Richard Strauss (the same),
also for the *Times;* and I must write specials on Vienna
(*Century Magazine*), and Prague for *Scribner's;* not to
mention articles on "Modern German Art" (which I
abominate) and one on Vermeer.

Of course, any reckless newspaper corre-
spondent could have taken on such a lot of
commissions, but the striking fact is that
Huneker was qualified to write with a degree
of critical authority on every one of the
subjects except the political one.

Such an output demanded fast writing;
and he wrote at a pace that only a journalist achieves: 5,000 words a day for long
stretches; a 6,000-word magazine article
once in six hours; and to cap all climaxes:

In Paris, where I went to write, I accomplished the
well-nigh crazy feat of writing 33,000 words from a
Thursday night to a Sunday morning (i.e., Monday
3:30 A.M.). Several days I wrote fourteen hours at a
stretch.

Full of spirit though he was, he flagged often under the incessant drive. His newspaper writing was all piecework, his book royalties were small, and the need of the dollar pursued him.

> I'm fagged with the theatre and music and travel. . . . . When you are in the saddle . . . . you will appreciate brain fag and the unutterable weariness that comes from 52 weekly repetitions. . . . . Some day my nerves will rebel. . . . . That will give me my nights free—free to toil.

Yet way toward the end, when natural fatigue was aggravated by illness, the old, boyish zest buoyed him on:

> My summer is lost. No music. No outings. Ten thousand words weekly. . . . . And hell and writer's cramp and I can't typewrite, I can't dictate. But oh! what a beautiful flow of language is gushing up from my subconsciousness, what a dazzling rainbow mist of vocables!

Such speed and such outwellings made for a fluent yet sinewy style. He had his theory, and gave it in comments on some of his younger friends; as, for example:

> Don't write with grave pauses, profound smirks and all the pompous silly amatory mean little reserva-

tions, attenuations, periphrases and involutions of your contemporaries. Far better an honest staccato phrase than a wilderness of sostenutos.

He never praised his own work, but he enjoyed the praise of others, especially the testimony of translation into other languages. He was inclined to undervalue himself, but in a long letter to H. L. Mencken he made a fair diagnosis, and, incidentally, supplied an honest staccato phrase:

No, I've not a drop of German blood in me. If I had I might possess more of what I once called The Will-to-Sit-Still (*Sitzfleisch*). I'm too Celtic, too centrifugal, as opposed to the centripetal Teuton too fickle, if too Catholic, and I'm a poor man at fifty-six. . . . . I'm Celto-Magyar—Pilsner and Donnybrook Fair.

It is a very intriguing Bohemian that appears in these *Letters* where he has for the moment quite forgotten the public. He is an eager lover of the things that are more excellent; versatile all the time, but some of the time an exact and exhaustive student; an overflowing spring of generous impulses, a sensitive and abiding friend; and a loyal lover. It must have been fun to know him.

One cannot quite imagine Mr. Higginson and Mr. Huneker in the same company. The Bostonian would doubtless, after escaping with a sigh of relief, have referred to the Bohemian as "very radical." It is just as well not to speculate on what the Bohemian, escaping with murmured expletives, would have called the Bostonian. No room has yet been built that would have held them both comfortably. Yet the country was big enough for both of them, and needs both their kinds, and is the better for both of their active, communicative lives.

XIV

The Younger Set and the Puritan Bogey

IT APPEARS that the welfare of the nation is threatened by a new menace. The danger is imminent, and the enemy is under attack from both flanks. According to the solicitous conservative, the college professor is undermining the foundations of society. He is talking about truth and the open mind. He is trying to base his opinions on the facts. He has the effrontery to say what he thinks about politics and international affairs and even about the market; with the result that some of the timorous abuse him, and the rest try to save the state by feeding him into contentment. At the same time, he is assailed from the left on the charge that he is already content. He is "a professorial guardian of colonial precedents," "an intellectual satrap," "a colonial inquisitor," "a doctor and saint of literature," "toneless, hopeless, crabbed, dreary, drab." Worst of all he is a Puritan.

This is mildly stimulating to the professor, who is not used to being taken seriously either for better or for worse. A gentle mauling relieves the monotony of his cloistered repose. What the reactionaries say fails to arouse in him anything but a hope that they are telling the truth—that if he is not red he is at least visibly tinged with pink. And what the newly wise say gratifies him by its proof that they are aware of him at all.

The younger set, as one of them calls the rest of them without indicating *de senectute* where old age begins, are just now making the professor the burden of an old song: the song begun in Revolutionary days, that American literature ought to be national, and that American writers and critics ought to be independent of Old World standards. It has echoed down the generations from Freneau to Whitman, and from Whitman via Hamlin Garland to the present day. One of

the features that bears witness to its genuine vitality is that it has always been chanted
as though it had just been composed. One
of the features that makes it pleasantly fresh
today is that it is now being sung *fortissimo*
by a chorus of young Americans whose composite derivation is obvious and recent, and
whose acquaintance with the country as a
whole has seldom taken many of them west
of Tenth Avenue; and, incidentally, they are
varying the harmony by building it over a
kind of anti-academic counterpoint.

The younger set are amiable incarnations
of the paradox they piously pursue. "It is
precisely because," they say, as they utter
Chestertonic platitudes that are of all things
unprecise because they are sweeping expressions of temperament whose sole charm lies
in their reckless unprecision. They preach
the gospel of joy, frowning the while as
desperately as the fiercest of boy bandits or
the grimmest of the Puritans at whom they
inveigh. No doubt they laugh betimes, but
the mention of laughter arouses them to
indignation at those who do not laugh.

They cannot enjoy the circus for the thought of those who have stayed at home. They may not like whiskey, but they drink in conscientious defiance of the Eighteenth Amendment. They devote themselves so intently to berating the living and blasting the dead that it is hard to find out what they really indorse. But it appears in the end that they indorse one another, and subscribe to the prejudices of their high priest, particularly to his obsessions about the Puritan and the professor.

As the younger set have never attempted a full-length portrait of the Puritan, their readers are left to infer that he is something quite American, compounded from the smugness of Cotton Mather, the austerity of Jonathan Edwards, the strident angularity of Shaw's Mrs. Dudgeon, and the gift of self-denial extended to others—denial typified in Anthony Comstock. It is a caricature, and not even a native one. Sir Toby's remark celebrated the case of Virtue versus Cakes-and-Ale only after it had been in court for generations. Ben Jonson took his fling;

Prynne and Collier gave new grounds for attack; Thomas Morton and Nathaniel Ward joined the fray in Massachusetts with books that too few have enjoyed; and so the apostolic succession has continued on both sides up to the tercentenary enthusiast who, for the moment, was for canonizing all his forefathers, and the modern anti-Puritan who is for putting them all in the pillory. At which point we come to the hostile assumption that Puritanism has one dominant and exclusive trait—a belief in ethical standards and a ruthless will to impose them on a recalcitrant world. It would be equally fair to retort that the anti-Puritan, not content with banning ethical standards from art, is dedicated to repudiating them in life; but the only rejoinder worth making is the friendly suggestion that the younger set when they feel most violent should substitute for Puritanism a word of their own coinage—Comstockery —and that when they want reinforcement they go to some other authority than the accumulating anthology of caricature. After all, Hawthorne has doubtless drawn a better

indictment against the Puritan than any
other American—his entire output amounts
to little more; and Matthew Arnold quite as
good a one as any other Englishman. *Culture
and Anarchy* presents the whole problem, and
one chapter, which need not be specified for
any cultured anarchist, the case against the
Hebraists.

Yet nothing simplifies life more pleasantly
than the experience of seeing only one thing
at a time. It is at the base of most passion and
most achievement. It accounts for love and
murder and high finance and war-heroism
and the grim zest of reformers and anti-
reformers. It also accounts for the word "precisely," and for freedom of generalization
that would be splendid if it were not funny.
For the younger set, in their hatred of the
Puritan, whenever they uncork the vials of
their wrath, where they keep him always in
pickle, he spreads out genii-like till he
clouds the heavens. Then they greet him
with shrill and prolonged outcries of which
Mr. Mencken gives an example in a commentary on the Puritanism of the South. It is

two-and-a-half pages long; it begins with, "It is, indeed, precisely," and it ends with:

> The only domestic art this huge and opulent empire knows is in the hands of Mexican greasers; the only native music it owes to the despised negro; its only genuine poet was permitted to die up an alley like a stray dog.

In the intervening pages the sole defects of the South that are not charged against the heaven-darkening specter are the evils of the one-crop system and the high temperature of Yuma, Arizona.

If people do not talk too hard it is measurably true that "What they don't know won't hurt them"; but when they do talk too hard, they serve themselves an ill turn by an avoidable betrayal of what they do not know. Thus, when Mr. Mencken states that

> Our great humourists, including even Mark Twain, have had to take protective colouration, whether willingly or unwillingly, from the prevailing ethical foliage, and so one finds them leveling their darts, not at the stupidities of the Puritan majority, but at the evidence of lessening stupidity in the anti-Puritan minority,

he makes the interesting revelation that he does not understand *Innocents Abroad* or *The Man That Corrupted Hadleyburg* or *Joan of Arc*, and that he has not read Mark Twain's "War Prayer" or his protest at the indignity done to the remains of George Holland or the controversy with Dr. Ament on the Boxer indemnities.

When Mr. Mencken comes to Whitman he dismisses him as "clearly before his time." What independent thinker is not? The inference is that Mr. Mencken does not wish to admit his admiration for Walt because he is resolved to be unhappy at all American literature. And the implication that possibly he does not care to acknowledge, or perhaps he does not know, that Whitman was the greatest Puritan of them all. Says Mr. Mencken bitterly:

It needed no official announcement to define the function and the office of the republic as that of an international expert in morals, and the mentor and exemplar of the more backward nations.

To which Whitman might have replied, had the years spared him: "It was *precisely* on this account that I once wrote,

Have the elder races halted,
Do they droop and end their lesson, wearied, over
there beyond the seas?
We take up the task eternal, and the burden, and the
lesson,
Pioneers, oh pioneers."

But Mr. Mencken's finest gesture is with reference to Emerson and the *Dial*. He has recently disposed of Emerson as "vague and empty" when he comes on some paragraphs quoted from the old quarterly, and applauds a passage on freedom of thought which appeared in its salutatory of 1840. But times have changed, he says:

As for the *Dial*, it was till lately, the very pope of orthodoxy, and jealously guarded the college professors who read it from the pollution of ideas.

There is a nice humor (or "humour," as Mr. Mencken, the iconoclast, would spell it) in this. For Mr. Mencken does not know that Emerson wrote the salutatory he cites; that Emerson was promoter and editor of that Boston *Dial* which faded away in 1844; and that the conservator of professorial innocence which has recently experienced a sea-change was not established until 1880.

When all's said and done, Mr. Mencken and his disciples of the younger set appear to a "professorial guardian of colonial precedents" to be a recrudescence of the New York Bohemians of seventy years ago. They were very aggressive, very unconventional, and very clever. They were so amiable that even that valiant conservative, William Winter, loved them in spite of his convictions. They achieved little in permanent literature but much in contemporary journalism; and they helped to retrieve the balance of the times. Their "prince," Henry M. Clapp, was certainly a man of less substantial performance than Mr. Mencken, though not inferior in his hatred of the Puritans. "Whenever I think of Boston," said Henry Clapp, "it makes me as ugly as sin."

The refrain of the anti-Puritans is rather like "Yankee Doodle" in its history and its appeal. The tune was an old one, and the words a ballad composite aimed in derision at a New England type. For a decade it was nothing more, until with the exploits at Concord and Lexington it became a rallying

The Younger Set and the Puritan Bogey

call for all the stalwarts of the colonies. So it has continued ever since; and so the anti-Puritan refrain stirs the pulse of the traditionalists as the scoffers pipe it from time to time. It needs no "Long live the younger set" from any professor to keep them alive, nor any vocal assurance that it seems no more than sane—though sometimes less than safe— to wish them old age and prosperity. They must press on in pursuit of their desperate design "to instruct the young, reform the old, correct the town, and castigate the age." Perhaps in time they will learn to turn the trick as cheerfully as did the Salmagundis and the Croakers, their earliest New York predecessors. In the meantime, we can recommend that they season their diet of prejudice with the salt of fact, and when they next have at us with their "Down with the Puritan and the professoriate," we can reply with Johnny Armstrong, best of sportsmen:

> I am a little hurt, but I am not slain,
> I'll lay me down for to bleed awhile,
>   And then I'll rise and fight with you again.

XV

Biography and the Personal Equation

I

THE use of such words as "criticism" and "biography" as though they were not specialized names for the same kind of product prevails in all likelihood partly because in one case the process is applied to books and in the other to personalities, and partly because most biographical writing falls so far short of what it ought to be. There is too little recognition of Hennequin's sage dictum that criticism is the science of the personal equation. Whether a man's real self is recorded in his living or in his writing makes no difference on the surface of the problem, and under the surface it makes only the difference that, as his living is mostly unconscious and his writing mostly calculated, the challenge to the critical powers of the biographer is doubled, and the problems of selection and evaluation many times multiplied.

The personal equations that Hennequin alluded to were those of the man written about and the man writing. Each is made up of more or less discoverable intellectual capacities, aesthetic predilections, and ethical prejudices or convictions. The highest common factor, whether of agreement or disagreement, is the chief determinant of the point of view, and the lowest common multiple of the two characters is the resulting biography, a product which depends chiefly on the acumen of the biographer and the honest candor with which he can pursue and complete his study. When the chronicler is a whole-souled disciple of the man chronicled, a Boswell's Johnson is turned out; a mutual hatred of smug, social taboos results in a Strachey's interpretation of a Florence Nightingale—we see her as through a glass starkly; an eager desire to pre-empt claims in the newly opened and undeveloped territory of psychoanalysis leads excursionists

like Brooks and Anthony to stake out and
offer stock in the Mark Twain silver mine or
the Margaret Fuller sheep ranch. And always, before the product is actually com-
pleted, a third personal equation must be
reckoned with—that of the reader. It is a
hard matter to write a good biography, and
it is, or ought to be, an intellectual adventure to read one; for to read one man's life is
to deal with two men's personalities, and to
pit a third against them both. For example—

II

About a decade ago was published Albert
Bigelow Paine's *Life of Mark Twain*—a Bos-
wellian work. The biographer spent four
years in almost constant company with his
subject. They were equally interested and
engrossed in the project. It was their joint
vocation. Every existing document was
studied, and every witness consulted. Paine
questioned, Twain answered, and a stenog-
rapher transcribed in full. Nothing lacked
in abundance of data. As to accuracy, the
only obstacle was the inventive memory of

the hero of the story for whom was gathering an old age in which he could best recall only the things that had not happened. This errantry was offset by the fact that the collaborators both knew of it, and the younger one was on guard against it. When it came to selection or inclusion of material, the two were equally undiscriminating, as much so as circumstantial biographers should be. Everything was grist for the mill, for time had already blown away the chaff, and there was nothing to conceal. Paine was as keen about Twain's billiards as he was about his books, and dwelt with the same fondness on his creative profanity that he did on his methods of more formal authorship, valuing them all as bricks and straw for the chronicle of a monumental personality. But when it came to recording the kaleidoscopic array of facts, Mark Twain contributed an artistic detachment to the story which served as an offset to the younger man's hero-worship, for though he was amiably self-regardful on the surface, in his inner thought he regarded himself as no less negligible than all the other "individuals of this infinitesimal race."

So the joint undertaking is a product of the biographer's regard for fact and the subject's sense of human values. Down through the 1,600 pages strides Mark Twain, working, loafing, talking, lecturing, joking, brooding; making fortunes and losing them; making friends and holding them; challenging the facts of life and speculating on its mystery, and coming to the end with the challenge not fully uttered and the speculation quite unanswered. It seemed fairly clear when the big work was published that no one need ever to revise the facts as a whole, or to be able to supplement them much. It is certain now that we need go nowhere else than to this work and the writings of Mark Twain from which it drew, and to the posthumous volumes which have appeared and are yet to appear. The facts are before us. The man who lived the life was the real author of the work, and the biographer was a transparent and only slightly magnifying medium. However, being the transparent medium that the biographer *in extenso* should be, he did little in the way of interpretation, seldom introducing his personality into the story, and even less often intruding his ideas. The personal equation of Mr. Paine hardly enters into the product. He undertook to keep it in abeyance, and succeeded about as well as a personal friend and admirer could be expected to. So he left all sorts of chances to the rest of us for all sorts of analyses and appraisals; and the chances have been by no means neglected.

III

Witness, for example, Mr. Howells' *My Mark Twain*, a series of reminiscences published in the very year of Mr. Clemens' death. The two had known and loved each other from young manhood, sometimes separated for longish intervals, but never completely losing contact. Mr. Howells made the start toward friendship with a sympathetic review of *Innocents Abroad*. From then to the end he was critic and adviser. His verdict convinced the author of *Tom Sawyer* that the boy-story was worth printing, and his published criticism put the seal of approval on the uniform edition of Mark Twain's works nearly a generation later. Few friendships have been built on a solider foundation or out of more strikingly complementary material. Both were disposed to face the facts of life and challenge existing conditions. They were both men of utmost probity of character, stalwart exponents of established morals.

But here the resemblance ceased. Mark Twain loved to be a figure in the public eye, shouted his doubts and forebodings from the housetops, and dared his hearers to disapprove. His white serge of later years, his ornate vocabulary of objurgation, and his violations of the drawing-room proprieties were all parts of his manner and his manners, which were calculated to display his contempt for the politer conventions of "the damned human race." But Mr. Howells was shy and reticent. Put them together and there could be only one result.

With his crest of dense red hair and the wide sweep of his flaming moustache, Clemens was not discordantly clothed in that sealskin coat, which afterward, in spite of his own warmth in it, sent the cold chills through me as I accompanied it down Broadway, and shared the immense publicity it won him.

Mr. Howells felt shivers and goose-flesh over and over again on the score of the irrepressible Mark, and always on grounds of taste rather than principle. It could not be otherwise for one who felt that all literature should be acceptable for all Victorian girlhood. Mark Twain's allegiance belonged to another monarch. "His Elizabethan breadth of parlance" and "his graphic touch" were always indulging in freedom which the reticent friend could not allow his fainter pencil even to illustrate. And Mr. Howells suffered the more when, in exposing his undisciplined guest to the keen edge of discreetly selected Cambridge acquaintances, he saw the Cantabridgians flinch as Mark's careless tread instinctively found out what Lowell goutily called "the tender foot of speechless dignities."

So the loyal friend spoke in tones of solid admiration, though he spoke with a deprecatory smile, and he sighed with relief when now and then one of his more fastidious friends accepted without reserve this "shirt-sleeved Charlemagne of empires new." Clemens in the eyes of Silas Lapham's creator was rather painfully lawless in small matters, bitter to malignancy in personal resentments, a wild tumult of rebellion against social stupidities and cruelties, but at the core exquisite, a man of tragic seriousness, of great, silent dignities. *My Mark Twain* was by title and nature a personal tribute which is only half read if Mr. Howells is not interpreted into every page.

IV

Mr. Van Wyck Brooks's volume on *The Ordeal of Mark Twain* is a book of an entirely different order. It is not written with the purpose of confining itself to accurate presentation of facts like Mr. Paine's voluminous work, or of indulging itself in an outpouring of affection, like Mr. Howells' heartfelt tribute. It is written to a thesis. It does not attempt to challenge or add a single fact, but it sets out to present an independent interpretation of what everyone can read in the life of Mark Twain and in his works.

There was a reason for Mark Twain's pessimism, a reason for that chagrin, that fear of solitude, that tortured conscience, those fantastic self-accusations, that indubitable self-contempt. It is an established fact, if I am not mistaken, that these morbid feelings of sin, which have no evident cause, are the result of having transgressed some inalienable life-demand peculiar to one's nature. . . . . That bitterness of his was the effect of a certain miscarriage in his creative life, a balked personality—an arrested development of which he was himself almost wholly unaware, but which for him destroyed the meaning of life.

This is the suppressed-desire thesis, based on "an established fact," says Mr. Brooks, "if I am not mistaken."

To develop this thesis is no light undertaking; and Mr. Brooks does not approach it lightly. On the contrary, he comes up to it, and progresses through it, and announces his pre-announced and oft-iterated conclusion with portentous solemnity. In 100,000 words his subject's social surroundings are presented, and his career surveyed. Mark

Twain, he says at great length, was once a boy with a normal boy's dislike to be washed behind his ears. When his mother, who loved him, bade him farewell at death's door, she bade him be a good boy. He shared in the exacting life of the western pioneer. He married a strong, gentle, orthodox, conventional wife, and lived in Hartford, Connecticut, for twenty Victorian years. He made and kept many friends. He was an exuberant play-boy in letters. He showed flashes of deep satiric power, but he deliberately chose not to make a complete revolt against the social order; and this for reasons of comfort and prudence. He died a pessimist and agnostic. There is no question as to all these assertions or allegations. Mr. Brooks has the documents for them, even for the satirist's choice of the easier course and the damaging reasons for it. And yet he leaves one unsatisfied at the vital link in the argument—the question of cause and effect:

Mark Twain was a frustrated spirit, a victim of arrested development, and beyond this fact, as we know from innumerable instances the psychologists

have placed before us, we need not look for an explanation of the chagrin of his old age.

Perhaps not, but again perhaps we do. We
remember Mr. Brooks's inadvertent qualify-
ing clause "if I am not mistaken," and we
wonder again. We look for light into his
own printed pages, as he has looked into
Mark Twain's, and find that his regular
approach to a problem is to say: "This is the
generally accepted opinion on the subject—
it must therefore be mistaken. For what
reasons?" It is a mode of thinking that
feeds on dissent, woos paradoxes, delights in
hidden meanings, and espouses new theories
on sight. It is the thinking of the "precisely" school. We remember now that in
an earlier volume Mr. Brooks reduced all
civilization to three men in a tub, and
America's coming of age to the maudlin ine-
briety of a youth who is at once celebrating
marriage and majority. Such a combination
of brilliant speech and unbridled generalization reminds us of the sane conclusion
that a Roman candle makes a brilliant light,
but it is a poor thing to go to bed by.

We find in Mr. Brooks the pomposity and fatuousness that he attributes to Whitman. But knowing even less than he does about unresolved complexes and suppressed desires, we are not even sure that he is wrong. We feel as Sidney Smith did about Macaulay, that we would thank God if we could be as cock sure of anything as he is of everything. And we look to the reading of his next book as a pleasant adventure, though an adventure which we shall be bound not to take too seriously.

V

It is not straining a point to say that the third of the personal equations, that of the reader, may also be found in print. It is what one finds in the writings of men like Lytton Strachey and Gamaliel Bradford, for their portraits are not as much biography in themselves as the impressions that biographies have produced on single observers. One looks at a portrait for the likeness, if the subject is a personal acquaintance, or for technical artistry if the subject is a stranger —in either case for skill in interpretation.

However, to use two of the author's favorite attributives, it is "curious" that "precisely" on these grounds Mr. Bradford's portraits are unsatisfying. The artist's personality that appears in these portraits is more insistent than impressive. As he confesses in the remarks prefatory to *American Portraits*, he has undertaken a vast historical painting which on the present scale will include no less than fifty-six heads. He seems to be striving in scale for the sober faithfulness of Washington Allston, but in manner for the vivacity of Barton's Chauve Souris curtain. He hopes to cover American history, but he covers it so thick with portraits that there is no sight of any background. The task needs the incisive powers of a Hogarth, but too often it falls to the hortatory methods of the Reverend Doctor Trusler, who published *Hogarth Moralized* for the edification of a godless and immoral public.

Thus the portrait of Mark Twain is bafflingly indeterminate. At the outset, says Mr. Bradford:

When I was a boy of fourteen, Mark Twain took hold of me as no other book had then, and few have since. . . . . I laughed till I cried. . . . . The criticism of life . . . . set me thinking as I had never thought before, and for several years colored my maturing reflection in a way that struck deep and lasted long.

This sounds like commendation; but at the end he declares:

It took years to shake off the withering blight which Mark's satire cast for me over the whole art of Europe. For years he spoiled for me some of the greatest sources of relief and joy.

This sounds like condemnation. Mr. Bradford may have had the latter statement in mind when he wrote the opening one; but if he did, he kept it so deep in the back of his mind that the reader feels that he put feet of clay on an image of gold as a kind of casual afterthought.

"As to his theoretical conclusions," says Mr. Bradford, "it may be said that they were nihilistic." It ought to be said that they were agnostic, that from the time when he became aware of his "reasoning powers" he labored painfully to save the faith he could not maintain from the reasoning that he could not gainsay. This was his tragedy written all through his later works, but to Mr. Bradford it is not so momentous as the early jocosities about medieval art. Mr. Howells wrote too truly in a book that Mr. Bradford never cites:

> It is in vain that I try to give a notion of the intensity with which he pierced to the heart of life; and the breadth of vision with which he compassed the whole world, and tried for the reason of things and then left trying.

As a generally accepted appraiser of personalities, Mr. Bradford invites an evaluation of his own gifts as a critic, not only because of the applause he is receiving, but because he is self-conscious to such a degree that even in his latest book he refers to himself as "an insignificant, impertinent, treacherous biographer." In his lack of the "simplicity and almost child-like candor" which he attributes to all his *Damaged Souls* except John Randolph, he raises a question as to the pertinence and significance of his portraits—to his method as well as his insight.

In his assembling of materials, if he is not impertinent, he is too often unpertinent and inconsecutive. In point of structure he seems to be so assured that consistency is the hobgoblin of little minds that he is not haunted by it even throughout the course of a single chapter. The sketch of Paine is an example. Paine is a rebel, and a rebel delights in destruction. Yet, he says, Paine preached nationality, co-ordination, co-operation, federal control. He espoused many of the reforms "which are now so accepted that we cannot imagine the world without them." This does not seem to be very destructive, but Mr. Bradford returns to his charge. He was disrespectful to George Washington, and to God. Yet "he affirmed and reaffirmed, with obvious honesty, his belief in God and his abiding and comforting hope of a future life." Once again the boat has gone on the wrong tack; so Mr. Bradford brings it about with the flat statement that Paine felt no awe and no reverence, and "had not an atom of religion in him."

There is little use in pursuing the point as a thesis, but this fine *non-sequitur* leads to

another defect in the Bradford method—
the extraordinary misuse of words. This is
the more striking in view of the biographer's
oft-declared respect for words. A common
gift of the *Damaged Souls* was their "facility,
if not felicity" with them. Barnum "made
words serve his purpose." Butler was "a
master of words." "Words with something
behind them make the man who prevails."
Yet Mr. Bradford's carelessness in diction is
egregious. To follow the commentary on
Paine's lack of religion: There was "no
longing, no craving, no aspiration, nothing
whatever of the mystic's high emotion and
all-absorbing love." Religion, apparently,
could exist only in him who was a mystic.
There are no varieties of religious experience.
Yet Mr. Bradford has no clearer conception
of mysticism than he has of religion, as the
next four words demonstrate: "Mystery? He
abhorred mystery." For the fundamental
experience of the mystic is not that he is
conscious of mystery, but that he is conscious of an ineffably clear perception of the
truth. It is not with these words alone, but
with the average run of abstract terms that

Mr. Bradford is repeatedly confused. One is tempted, in his own phraseology, when he resorts to abstract words, "to regard these insinuating agents with extreme skepticism."

This verbal insecurity, moreover, is only a symptom of something at the basis of his criticism: his general measure of values and his failure to establish any secure platform for himself. He regards himself as a rather startling liberal—"Oh, what fun it is to be a rebel!"—though he is only a follower in the ranks, and even at that an intermittent one: "Some of us occasionally like to think new thoughts and step out of the beaten track, and we like one who makes us do these things." Yet he is so little of a rebel or an innovator that he likes also to be mildly shocked at divagations from the open road which he is willing to witness but not to record, acknowledging a covert pleasure in reminiscences which he has not the courage to share: "I wish I could embellish these decorous pages with the gay adventures of the fair Madame X in the crowded inn at Rotterdam."

When he exclaims, "Oh, what fun it is to be a rebel!" he implies that he has had some experience at this diversion; but as he goes on to characterize a rebel in the abstract, he shows that he has never been one nor intimately known one. It is a straw man he sets up. His rebel is the mischief-maker of history. Rebellion is a huge, practical joke. It is boisterous, destructive, humorless jollity, and the rebel is the thick-skinned convention smasher who can go on his way "untroubled by the criticism and abuse of spite and malice, indeed rather stimulated by them." This fancy picture bears almost no relation to actual rebels. The iconoclasts one knows have been moved to utterance and action by conditions they could not endure. They have soberly undertaken to set them right. Sensitive as Shylock at the expression of public scorn, they have been goaded to extravagance by criticism and abuse, and have suffered the tortures which come with being damned. Mr. Bradford says that Satan and Prometheus are "the great ideal rebels." Yet even they, as I recall them, do not seem to have reveled in the cheery irresponsibility which he ascribes to all their kind. Mr. Bradford was thinking of cynics, skeptics, journalistic radicals. He was writing with Tom Paine in mind, but he used a term which should apply equally to Paine and Washington and John Brown.

When Mr. Bradford declares further that "some of us occasionally like to think new thoughts and step out of the beaten track," he suggests again that he is speaking out of his experience. But a careful reading forces the conclusion that he is writing tolerantly from observation. There is no trace of new thought—in the sense of original or even independent thought—about family or school or market or church or state in all his pages. The canons of a Victorian America are finalities to him. He quotes Aaron Burr, and requotes him: "On full investigation it will be discovered that there is scarcely a departure from order but leads to or is indissolubly connected with a departure from morality." This harmonizes happily with his statement, a propos of

Randolph of Roanoke, that it is the essence
of conservatism "to hate change, to love
quiet, to seek repose." Of our "Constitution"
he states without argument that the most
important element is "the original principle
of state vitality." It is a broad thesis. Does
he really think so, has he thought through
what the statement means, or is he merely
saying one of the things echoed by those
who hate change, even of the habitual platitudes? It is neither a new thought nor a
rebellious one.

Whether it is Paine's whole-souled admiration of Mark Twain we have to reckon
with or Howells' semiapologetic devotion
or Brooks's psychoanalytic prepossessions or
Bradford's unconsciously disguised conserva-
tisms, the problem is the same—to understand the image which is displayed by understanding something of the lens through
which it is projected. Mr. Strachey, who
has earned the right to dogmatize on the
subject if anyone has, maintains that:

A biography should either be as long as Boswell's
or as short as Aubrey's. The method of enormous

and elaborate accretion which produced the *Life of Johnson* is excellent, no doubt; but, failing that, let us have no half-measures; let us have the pure essentials of a vivid image, on a page or two, without explanations, transitions, commentaries, or padding. This is what Aubrey gives us; this, and one thing more—a sense of the pleasing, anxious being who, with his odd alchemy, has transmuted a few handfuls of orts and relics into golden life.

If this be so, if even in his page or two Aubrey creeps in to transmute and alchemize, we would better have room for the intermediate scales of the Stracheys and the Bradfords and Howells's and Brooks's as well. Short of the tabloided entries in *Who's Who*—and not always even there—we can never be free in biography from the complex problem of the personal equation.

XVI

Pessimism and the Critical Code

COLD fact is always bewildering, coming as it does into conflict with comfortable preconception; and the rising generation of critics are having an unusually hard time because the facts of today are unusually cold. The new arbiters of taste are passing through the experience of an average Freshman with the baffling revelations of "survey" courses. When he learns in physiology that he has two hundred and odd bones in his precious body he is scared stiff. He tiptoes about for days in the fear of compound fracture; but gradually re-assurance returns as nothing happens when whole classes descend the stairways, defying gravitation as they step from precipice to precipice without a casualty. He is saved through works. When, however, he comes to evolution and the codfish, salvation is not so easily achieved. He learns that the codfish lays 2,000,000 eggs, more or less, of which only two come to maturity. It seems to him a fearful and stupid piscatorial waste—proof enough that there is no design in earthly affairs. There is no God. It does not comfort him to think that if the waste did not occur the ocean would soon be packed with cod. The excess should never have been laid. No God worth respecting would ever work his will by the trial-and-error method. Not having any personal experience to fall back on, he throws up his hands. Works fail; he has no faith. "Two million eggs!" he says. "Well, I'll be damned!" And to that cheerful expectation he resigns himself.

This pessimistic resignation works itself off variously in the prevailing thought of the day. It furnishes a bond of happy union for practical statesmen, returned soldiers, red radicals and black-browed conservatives, women who do not believe in marriage and men who do not believe in women, sopho-mores, anti-religionists and dyspeptics. Even Stuart Sherman, in a recent article on "The

Point of View in American Criticism,"
dwelling with his usual muscular felicity
on the growth of a national consciousness,
hails with satisfaction the healthy pessimism of the era. It is the usual point of
arrival for any discussion of the literary
self-consciousness of America, too. But there
is something still to be said on American
literature's attitude toward itself, which is
culminating now in the popular confection
of pessimism *à la mode*.

I

The sense of manifest destiny, and the
irresponsible optimism to which this sense
gave rise, began to find voice in America
even before the Revolution. One recalls
Crêvecoeur's much-quoted passage on the
"race of men whose labors and posterity will
one day cause great changes in the world,"
and the 1758 almanac of Nathaniel Ames, in
which he looked forward to the times, after
"the obscene howl" of the wild beasts
should have ceased forever, when "the
stones and trees will dance together at the

music of Orpheus, the rocks will disclose their hidden gems and the inestimable treasures of gold and silver will be broken up."

He addresses us:

O ye unborn inhabitants of America, should these alphabetical letters remain legible when your eyes behold the sun after he has rolled the seasons round for two or three centuries more you will know that in *Anno Domini* 1758 we dreamed of your times.

With American independence the twin fallacy of magnificent isolation, to which some of the old guard are still defiantly clinging, became vocal in epic outbursts, particularly of the Hartford wits. But even while Dwight was adjuring mankind to

See this glad world, remote from every foe,
From Europe's mischief and from Europe's woe,

Freneau was confessing to the strength of a transatlantic cable more binding than any to be laid under water, in his protests at "Literary Importation":

Can we never be thought to have learning or grace,
Unless it be brought from that horrible place
Where tyranny reigns with her impudent face?

And Barlow, Polonius-like, was protesting too much in behalf of the model of republicanism just put on exhibition, which each land was to "imitate, each nation join."

It is an old story that this state of happy complacency could not last long; that the Old World would not permit it. Trumbull resented in behalf of his townsmen that, when their ardent genius poured the bold, sublime, English critics carped at the style and nibbled at the rhyme, and Halleck was annoyed that they not only wrote from the other side, but

> . . . . paid us friendly visits to abuse
> Our country and find food for the reviews.

Moreover, to make matters worse, while the United States were passing into their national adolescence, there came the bitter sense that they actually offered a fair, broad target for European shafts. With the close of the War of 1812 and the restimulation of British disfavor, Americans deplored the very characteristics which they hated to have mentioned by foreigners. Halleck confessed to the vulgarism of urban pseudo-culture and the Yankee shrewdness of the man on the farm. Whittier, in retrospect, deprecated the decadence of the *unco guid*,

> . . . . fearful of the Unseen Powers,
> But grumbling over pulpit tax and pew rent,
> Saving as shrewd economists, their souls,
> And winter pork, with the least possible outlay
> Of salt and sanctity.

The Tory group, skeptical as to the whole theory of the republican government, threw up their hands in despair at what John Howard Payne's patron called "the desolating effects of democracy," and the self-consciously cultured—socially aristocratic, but politically impotent—shuddered at the new American commoner, the irrepressible,

> . . . . backwoods Charlemagne of empires new,
> Who, meeting Caesar's self, would slap his back,
> Call him "Old Horse," and challenge to a drink.

Almost all conspired to encourage by their indignant sensitiveness the "certain condescension in foreigners" at which Lowell later made his voluble protest, but which will never entirely disappear until Americans learn entirely to ignore it. And because in the years leading up to the Civil War the Olympian gift of imperturbability was left out of the American make-up, hypersensitiveness and self-blame combined to pester gawky and introspective Young America, the hypersensitiveness running all the way from Dwight's wrath at English malicious misrepresentation (because a certain traveler attributed chestnut trees instead of maples to some New Hampshire mountain interval) to the fine dignity of Irving's protest at *English Writers on America*, and the self-blame rising from the *Salmagundi* and *Croaker* papers and Halleck's "Fanny" and "Connecticut" to the unhappy climax of Cooper's *Homeward Bound* and *Home as Found*.

II

The lack of self-confidence to which all this palaver bore pathetic witness yielded its natural fruit in literature. As a rule, the only literary solicitude in the States was that Americans should write competently and in established modes. From Freneau's graduation at Princeton in 1770 to Longfellow's at

Bowdoin fifty-odd years later, commencement orators had gloried in the future of our letters. The same God who was presiding over our manifest destiny, and to whom we touchingly inscribed our trust on a debased silver dollar, was assumed to be an active patron of the arts. There was the beginning of a feeling that our writers should confine their attention to native themes. Tyler and Dunlap in dramatic prologues prided themselves on having done so, but only the profiles of the plays were American and the whole bone and sinew of them were English. Longfellow thought that the matter of indigenous material could be overstressed:

It is not necessary that the war whoop should ring in every line and every page be rife with scalps, tomahawks and wampum. Shade of Tecumseh, forbid!

Beneath the entire half-century was the assumption—sometimes tacit, sometimes expressed, but never gainsaid—that the best to be hoped for was the approximation of English models. American poets should

. . . . bid their lays with lofty Milton vie,
Or wake from moral themes the moral song,

And shine with Pope, with Thompson and with
  Young,
This land her Swift and Addison shall view,
The former honors equalled by the new;
Here shall some Shakespeare charm the rising age,
And hold in magic chains the listening stage,
A second Watts shall strike the heavenly lyre,
And other muses other bards inspire.

The harvest of such hopes was a crop
of Anglo-Americans; Brown, the American
Godwin, a Bryant for a Wordsworth, a
Cooper for a Scott, an Irving for an Addison-
Goldsmith; a generation of Byronic imita-
tors, a transcendental school building on
what Wordsworth and Coleridge and Carlyle had derived and transmitted from the
Germans; and a sentimental school which
wrote, as Beers has so cogently stated, of

. . . . a needlework world, a world in which
there was always moonlight on the lake and twilight
in the vale; where drooped the willow and bloomed
the eglantine, and jessamine embowered the cot of the
village maid; where the lark warbled in the heaven
and the nightingale chanted in the grove 'neath the
mouldering, ivy-mantled tower . . . . a world in
which there were fairy isles, enchanted grottos, peris,
gondolas, and gazelles.

In short, the gemmy and albuminous world of the "Albums" and "Gems" and "Gifts" and "Tokens" and "Offerings."

III

In the natural course of events, literary criticism followed creative writing even of this diluted sort. With it came the expression of judgment applied to literature as a whole, as in *Representative Men;* and the censorship of American literature, as in *The Literati*. It was for Emerson to protest at listening abjectly "to the courtly muses of Europe," and it was for Poe to mock at the domestic puffery which betrayed "the pride of a too speedily assumed literary freedom." In this contrast lies much of what has followed in the later generations. For, though the two men spoke within sound of each other, each was speaking very pertinently to his own audience: Emerson to rouse the timid scholastic group to some degree of initiative and self-reliance; and Poe to persuade the bumptious pot-boiling paragrapher and the public who would read him, not to like stupid books simply because their stupidities were American. Between the two Lowell held the mean and packed into the *Fable for Critics* more memorable judgments on his contemporaries than any other American has ever done in equal space.

In the English writing and English reading world the tendency to "wake from moral themes the moral song" was never stronger than in these mid-century decades. In this country Poe was almost alone in apostasy. Emerson mourned that "Shakespeare led an obscure and profane life," and that Goethe was "incapable of self-surrender to the moral sentiment." Hawthorne declared that it was a mistake "relentlessly to impale a story with its moral" yet usually stuck his pin visibly through the butterfly. Melville escaped, though a little shamefacedly, in *Typee,* and had his fling at the contemporary reviewers in what he made them say of Pierre's writings: "This writer is unquestionably a highly respectable youth"; "He is blameless in morals and harmless throughout." Thus the current of indorsement ran, finding its most substantial critical and creative expositor in Howells, who wanted to be a realist, though of the sort who would not cause the blush of shame to rise upon the maiden's cheek, and who felt the presence of Mark Twain's ribald letters in his desk as if they were a sort of ethical nitroglycerine.

Whitman's relations to both these doctrines were perfect expressions of the democratic movement which was fulfilled in himself and Lincoln and Grant. He was out of sympathy with the old niceties and the old taboos which accompanied them. He felt no more interest in Poe's aesthetic thesis than he felt for the actual rhymes of the jingle man. Poe's verses to him were "poems distilled from foreign poems"; his tales had no relevance to the "divine average." He welcomed—and capitalized—Emerson's indorsement of his self-reliance, but bettered the instructions of his elder by ignoring his cautions against violations of "good morals." He was repudiated in his country because he smelled of the barnyard rather than of the conservatory, and he was welcomed in England, as Mark Twain and Joaquin Miller were, because the Old World was more attracted by indigenous American growths than by provincial potted plants. In cultural taste America was still timid, and in ethical taste still largely dominated by Cotton Mather and Jonathan Edwards.

IV

However, since the nineties, as everyone knows, a thousand causes have conspired to change all that, in an overturn of critical judgment of which we are even now feeling the full force. As recently as 1902 Bliss Perry, in his *Study of Prose Fiction*, declared that the American novel was free from equivocal morality, that "people who want the sex novel and want it prepared with any literary skill have to import it from across the water," and that, "though American fiction may not be national and may not be great, it will at least have the negative virtue of being clean." Then he went on at once to prove how far he was from having the prophetic habit of mind by showing that he failed utterly to see any connection between this negative virtue and the interesting—or he might have thought ominous —sign that wherever American novelists were gathering together the talk was certain to center about men like Tourgenieff and Tolstoi, Flaubert and Daudet, Bjornson and d'Annunzio. Yet within a dozen years, and inevitably, the influence of the Continentals had become so urgent that the National Institute of Arts and Letters in one of their annual meetings, moved by the conservative element, went on record in protest against the morbid tendencies of contemporary American dramatists and novelists.

So here we are; and it is a normal, but none the less half-amusing, aspect of the situation that the current anti-Puritan criticism of today insists on expressing itself not merely in terms of emancipation but in shrill and hysterical cries of defiance of the old régime. On the moralistic side I have nothing to say now, for the issue is clearly defined and the old ethical standards, for better or for worse, are in the hands of the

Pessimism and the Critical Code

Babbitts and the Mores, the Shoreys and the Shermans. But there is another side of Puritanism, which is quite as momentous and on which the issue seems as yet to be quite undefined—and that is in the matter of romantic optimism.

I know of no other two words that have been so abused in recent years as "Puritanism" and "optimism." In their fates they are the choicest illustrations of one of the most popular of modern indoor sports—that of distorting the meaning of an old and tried term, and then of applying it in abusive ways to people one despises or distrusts. So Puritanism has come to connote the incarnation of a sort of universal Eighteenth Amendment, and optimism a pusillanimous refusal to face the facts of life. The cry is raised against Praise-God Barebones and Pollyanna, and the would-be Delphic manger-snappers, whom E. A. Robinson has so nicely characterized, take it out with equal zest on sadness and gladness, on Hebraism and Hellenism. If one is to be in the latest intellectual mode he must arrogate to himself a "healthy pessimism."

[279]

V

As one who regards himself neither as a pessimist nor altogether as a nincompoop, I have been successively abashed, ruffled, and bewildered by the cheerful chorus of despair until a little reading and a little meditation have convinced me that the singers swelling the chorus do not know the meaning of the words of the oratorio—as though the reiterated "All we-e-e, like sheep," were a hymn in praise of mutton. As I understand them—and I find almost no exceptions and none that need to be taken seriously—the "healthy pessimist" is not a pessimist at all—for optimism and its antonym have to do with ultimate ends rather than with immediate conditions—but simply the type of Diogenes who thinks that he is willing to see what his lantern reveals, although he much prefers to see the things that hide in darkness and that are revealed only by artificial light.

With a great deal of stage business he glances about him and discovers what he regards as the hitherto unnoticed fact that all is not right with the world. He fails to realize that in the first two-thirds of recorded history the main social achievement, after the creation of a king and the installation of a priest, was the formulation of a myth to account for human unhappiness—as the legends of Prometheus or of Adam and Eve— and that it was an intense conviction that all was not right with the world that made the Puritan the manner of man he was. The sudden shock of discovery that the times are out of joint fills him with disgust for childhood, laughter, and sunlight, and with contempt for the cheap optimism of the mistaken souls in this vale of tears who have not left all hope behind. Dulness and stupidity become his particular aversions. He is irritated by the vast majority of unthinking people who perhaps ought to be filled with despair, but who, as a matter of fact, are having a very good time with life, their glands being in stable equilibrium.

After all, the apostles of gloom are only part of a generation who have been like a devout and comfortable crowd assembled in a cathedral square, suddenly and shockingly converted into a frightened mob and dispersed into every blind alley within easy running distance. In the meanwhile the dust of dogma has been so stirred by breezes and winds and gales and tornadoes of fact that it is almost impossible to keep one's eyes open and see the truth. For the facts at the moment sometimes obscure it and sometimes belie it. So it is that the men who can achieve the paradox of seeing most clearly by looking within, open themselves to the indictment of being blinkers, blind fools, impracticable idealists, irresponsible optimists—the vocabulary of invective is too familiar to repeat. But in the midst of the confusion one can hear the outcries of the healthy pessimists who have kept their eyes open only to get them filled with dust, and who mistake their tears of irritation for spontaneous grief.

This is the most strident note in American literary criticism today, the latest chapter in the unfolding story of American literary self-consciousness. The insistence against both Hebraism and Hellenism—a simultaneous

fight on grimness and "Sunny Jimness"—
is an antidote against the moralism and the
sentimentalism of the recent past; and the
somberly realistic approach to the life of
today is a lusty challenge to a muddled
democracy in the midst of a muddled world.
A lost urchin on a city street no doubt
regards himself as a lost soul for the moment;
but happily, in fact, he is only a bewildered
and panic-stricken pseudo-pessimist.

Index

Index

Index

PRINTED IN THE U.S.A.